Global Reordering

Series Editors

How is the global order changing, and why? The contemporary dynamics of the global political economy and global security in the twenty-first century are experiencing a series of fundamental transitions, which are challenging and transforming the existing global order. These dynamics are reshaping relations between and within different categories of actors such as states, club forums, international organizations, transnational policy communities, private sector agencies and corporations, and civil society organizations. At the same time, processes of global reordering have led to the emergence of new issue areas and policy problems that the existing landscape of national, regional, and global governance is struggling to effectively address. The Centre for the Study of Globalisation and Regionalisation (CSGR) at the University of Warwick has been home, since 2011, to a major EU funded research project on Global Reordering. With 16 partners from across the world, the project has focussed on how European interests, objectives, and modes of governance might influence the way in which a post-unipolar global order takes shape. Global Reordering seeks to build on this research agenda, and also expand it by moving beyond just a European focus towards a truly global perspective. Global Reordering invites manuscript submissions based on innovative empirical research that is theoretically-informed and is relevant for contemporary policy debates. The series welcomes proposals for authored monographs, edited volumes and short length Pivots. Key areas include: changing modes of global governance and multipolarity; global public policy networks; emerging powers and multipolar alternatives; regions and regionalism; as well as regional and global leadership.

More information about this series at
http://www.springer.com/series/15015

Ray Kiely

# The Rise and Fall of Emerging Powers

## Globalisation, US Power and the Global North-South Divide

palgrave
macmillan

Ray Kiely
School of Politics and International Relations
Queen Mary University of London
London, United Kingdom

Global Reordering
ISBN 978-3-319-34011-1 ISBN 978-3-319-34012-8 (eBook)
DOI 10.1007/978-3-319-34012-8

Library of Congress Control Number: 2016949256



Cover illustration: Détail de la Tour Eiffel
© nemesis2207/Fotolia.co.uk

Printed on acid-free paper

This Palgrave Macmillan imprint is published by Springer Nature
The registered company is Springer International Publishing AG Switzerland

# Previous Books by Ray Kiely

The BRICs, US 'decline' and global transformations, Palgrave, 2015.

Rethinking Imperialism, Palgrave Macmillan, 2010.

The New Political Economy of Development, Palgrave Macmillan, 2007 (Korean translation published 2011).

Empire in the Age of Globalisation: US Hegemony and Neo-liberal Disorder, 2005.

The Clash of Globalisations: Neo-liberalism, the Third Way and 'Anti-Globalisation', 2005.

Industrialisation and Development: A Comparative Analysis, 1998.

The Politics of Labour and Development in Trinidad, 1996.

Sociology and Development: the Impasse and Beyond, 1995.

# Acknowledgements

Thanks to all at the School of Politics and International Relations at Queen Mary University of London, particularly Rick Saull. Outside of QMUL, Andrew Gamble, Leo Panitch, Alfredo Saad-Filho and Andy Sumner were particularly important sources of support and inspiration for this project. In accordance with an invented tradition of mine, for this project I have mainly been listening to REM (especially the 1980s era), Yucatan, the Beastie Boys and, as always, Low. Thanks also as always to Emma, Will and Ella.

# Contents

# List of Tables

CHAPTER 1

# Introduction

**Abstract** This chapter sets up the debate and structure for the rest of the book. It shows how the book will examine both international relations (IR) theories and development theories in order to consider the rise and fall of the South, and specifically how modernisation and dependency approaches will be used as framing devices to contextualise and analyse the discussion.

**Keywords** China • BRICs, global South • US hegemony • Emerging markets crisis

Until as recently as 2015, there was (and still is) a growing sense that we are witnessing something of a transformation in the international order. Central to this contention are two distinct but often related issues, namely, that of the rise of a new South led by the BRIC[1] (Brazil, Russia, India and China) countries, and the decline of the USA (albeit just a few years after being described by some as a unipolar power or empire). This small book accepts that there has to some extent been a rise of (parts of) the South, but suggests that this is more limited than is often claimed, and indeed goes further and suggests that the discourse of the rise of emerging powers is slowly—and rightly—giving way to one which focuses on a new *emerging markets crisis*. In order to contextualise this argument, the book


R. Kiely, *The Rise and Fall of Emerging Powers*,
DOI 10.1007/978-3-319-34012-8_1

suggests that the decline of the USA has been seriously exaggerated, and indeed that there is a close connection between the "rise" of the South, its limits (and partial "fall"), and the character of US power in the international order.

While some general arguments will be made to illustrate this case, the main focus will be on the question of political economy rather than geopolitics (or global governance). This is not to deny that geopolitics are very important, but the narrower focus on political economy is justified because much of the case around the rise of the South, and specifically China, and decline of the West, and specifically the USA, focuses on the supposed economic decline of the USA and economic rise of the South, the BRICS (including South Africa), and above all China. It is here that the book makes two distinctive, but related arguments. First, the political economy of "globalisation"[2] reflects less the decline of the USA and more the USA' ***continued but distinctive leadership of the international order***[3]. This is an argument which has been developed by some writers from different theoretical positions, including Nye (2015), Ikenberry (2014) and Beckley (2011/2012) from a liberal internationalist position, and Panitch and Gindin (2012) and Saull (2012) from a broadly undogmatic (and perhaps unorthodox) marxian[4] position. What is distinctive about US leadership is that in some respects it is one that is integrationist, as it attempts to incorporate other states into a liberal international order. Seen in this way, liberal internationalists are correct to identify interdependence as a central characteristic of the current international order. On the other hand, my second argument however, develops and in some respects cuts across this first argument, because—as will become clear in what follows—while there is a tendency towards integration, we need to identify in some detail the specific forms of integration that occur and in particular shows how these are characterised by ***unevenness and inequality***. We need to be clear here that this unevenness should not be confused with incompleteness, and rather show how unevenness is a product of cumulative inequality, rather than being a simple residual phenomenon which will be overcome through a process of catch-up and convergence. These very abstract and general points will be developed further in what follows, both generally, and in relation to the specific focus of this book, which is the alleged rise (and fall) of the South in recent years. On the face of it, the story of the recent rise would seem to suggests that interdependence has also given rise to convergence, but in what follows I will in fact argue that that there are good reasons why this supposed rise was based on a one-sided discourse, and even more, that we are now moving into a new period where we can talk less about the rise of emerging powers, and more about an emerging markets crisis. In doing so, the book will draw on both detailed empirical material and theoretical approaches from both international relations (IR) and development theory. In particular, in terms of theory, the book will suggest that notions of core and periphery in the international order remain useful concepts which, despite some problems, capture some of the realities of the changing international and global order. Concepts of core and periphery are often derived from world systems theory (Wallerstein 1974), and some versions of dependency theory, especially early underdevelopment theory (Frank 1969). There are some serious problems with these approaches and, I will suggest in the next chapter, with more recent approaches which draw on "global history" (Pomeranz 2001; Hobson 2004). In particular, there is a tendency to argue that the world is composed of a rather static hierarchical order, in which changes are "explained" by the overall needs of a hierarchical system. This is a functionalist argument which fails to deal with the specifics of change. When such approaches do recognise change, it is often through drawing on further spurious arguments, such as the idea that Asia has historically dominated the international order for all but the period from the early nineteenth century to the present, and now we are returning to a "normal" era of Asian hegemony (Frank 1998; Arrighi 2007). This again tends towards a view of history in which change is supposedly explained only through historical cycles, the specifics of which are lost in the analysis, and the implicit content of which is highly questionable. In particular, one of the secondary arguments in this book is to question the view that (insofar as it exists) Chinese hegemony is or would be more progressive than US hegemony. At the same time, this book does not accept the position of the liberal internationalists, insofar as it does not offer a normative apology for US hegemony. While this is secondary to the analytical account that follows, it should be clear that US hegemony is problematic and does indeed promote hierarchies and inequalities in the international order, even while it simultaneously promotes integration. What should be clear in what follows is that the integration that the USA promotes is both uneven and unequal, and indeed does lead to the promotion of cores and peripheries in the international order. This might not be the intention of US policymakers, even in problematic cases such as military intervention, which can be analysed in terms of integrating supposed non-integrators into "globalisation" (Barnett 2004). However, given the uneven and combined development of global capitalism, in which some countries, locations and regions develop through a process of cumulative causation

(Kiely 2010), US hegemony often serves to relatively marginalise as much as integrate.

This argument would appear to be problematic given the rise of a number of large, and significant countries from the South in recent years. However, in the chapters that follow I will show how this rise has taken place within a wider context of uneven and combined development, and that the rise of the BRICs and fall of the USA was limited, and we are now entering a period of crisis for the South. Indeed, the 2008 financial crisis will be an important part of the analysis that follows. Much of the story of the rise of the South focused on the South's seemingly rapid recovery, from 2010 onwards, in contrast to both the US crisis in 2008 and the Eurozone crisis from 2010 onwards. However, this book will argue that we are now entering a third phase of this crisis, and this is a crisis of emerging markets. Now of course this is a problem for the USA, and insofar as we might talk about US decline, this might refer to the US state's seeming incapacity to manage the fallout from the 2008 crisis. However, in contrast to approaches which imply that the US decline is also China's rise, and that the South has in effect delinked from the global North, it will be argued that this is a problem for all states and economies in the international order, including for the BRIC countries and the rest of the South.

This book therefore aims to do the following:

1. It questions the view that there has been an inexorable rise for the South, led by China and the other BRIC countries.
2. It questions the view that there has been a straightforward decline in US leadership in the international order.
3. It argues that the focus on analysis of the rise of emerging powers should now give way not only to an understanding of the limits of their rise, but also to an understanding of the growing crisis in so-called emerging markets and the South.

The book carries out these tasks in six chapters. Following this introduction (Chap. 1), the next chapter (Chap. 2) will provide a brief introduction to the idea of the rise of the South in recent years. It will then go on to examine the ways in which a number of theories of IR have attempted to explain this rise, and examine how implicit within these approaches is a particular understanding of development. The chapter will argue that, while in many respects problematic, the old development debate cast in terms of modernisation versus dependency theory remains a useful one, not least for analysing "the rise and fall of the South" in recent years. The chapter's final section provides an initial and strictly preliminary illustration of this argument through a brief assessment of the BRICs and the South in the period up to 2008, suggesting that the question of desirability or undesirability of a new Chinese or BRIC hegemony is less significant than the fact that the rise of China and the BRICs and so-called transformation of the international order have been exaggerated. This final argument is then considered in depth in the rest of the book, focusing on the periods both prior to and after the 2008 financial crash. Chapter 3 starts by considering the question of globalisation, focusing in particular on the rise of multinational companies and global production networks. The chapter then considers whether these developments have led to some degree of convergence in the international economy through the diffusion of capitalism across the globe. The idea of a rising South can be considered one significant part of this process of diffusion. But the next section will qualify this argument, first by comparing US profitability overseas with US foreign debt obligations, and showing how the former is greater than the latter. The explanation for this seeming paradox will be sought through a detailed empirical consideration of corporate ownership, in order to highlight the continued dominance of US (corporate) power in the international order. This discussion will then be used to return to the question of the theoretical dialogue outlined in Chap. 2, namely, the question of modernisation and dependency. Chapter 3 will therefore explicitly question the view that the USA is in decline and that the rise of the BRICs is challenging US hegemony. However, as has already been stated, some argue that the story of the rise of the BRICs and fall of the USA has intensified since the financial crisis of 2008, and Chap. 4 considers this question in some depth. The chapter first introduces this argument before subjecting it to critical scrutiny. Following previous work (Kiely 2015: Chap. 5), the chapter shows how the emerging markets boom rested on a number of specifics (Chinese–US interdependence, primary commodity booms in the rest of the South, capital flows to the South) and how, after the crisis, recovery in the South also rested on a number of factors (capital flows to the South, renewed high commodity prices, China's stimulus), which I previously argued were increasingly coming to an end. This chapter further develops and updates this story, and shows how the period from around 2013, but especially 2015 onwards, has seen the post-crisis recovery in the South come to an end. In particular, primary commodity prices have fallen, growth is slowing down and is coming to an end, capital flows are now shifting back to the North, and China's stimulus programme has run out of steam and growth in the lead economy among the BRICs has slowed down significantly. Indeed, we will see that some argue that China is entering a period of serious economic turmoil, one already faced by a number of countries in the South including some BRIC countries (and Brazil and Russia in particular). In other words, the emerging markets boom has given way to a growing emergency markets slowdown and possibly a crisis. Chapter 5 moves from an analysis of relations between states to one that focuses on inequality, not only within and between states, but also between peoples across and within states. The chapter briefly focuses on different approaches to international inequality and poverty (see also Kiely 2015: Chap. 6), and then moves on to present and discuss new data on inequality within countries and between peoples. It will then analyse this data to again put the question of modernisation and convergence in the international order into some kind of wider context, showing how most people living in absolute poverty or chronic insecurity remain in the global South. Finally, the long concluding chapter will bring the arguments together to discuss the key themes of the book, and in particular it will look at US power and IR theory and globalisation and uneven and combined development, and revisit the question of the growing shift from boom to bust in the global South.

This is my second book which deals with these issues (see Kiely 2015), and there are some small areas of repetition and overlap with parts of the previous work. However, this book is distinctive in three ways. First, it draws on significantly new data, especially on corporate ownership (Chap. 3), on the unfolding crisis in the South (Chap. 4) and on poverty and inequality (Chap. 5). Second, it develops in much greater empirical depth the details and argument concerning the growing crisis in the South, not least because of this new data now available. Third, this book has much greater analytical depth because there is far more discussion of how the rise and fall of the South can be located within wider frameworks drawn from theories of both IR and development. I now turn to a consideration of these issues, starting with the third question in the next chapter.

## Notes

1. The BRICs is a term coined by Jim O' Neill in 2001 to refer to Brazil, Russia, India, and China, and was largely used to refer to potential opportunities in those countries for investors looking for lucrative returns. The

term was, however, taken up by these countries, with the start of annual BRIC summits, which was then expanded to include South Africa, and thus become the BRICS. This is discussed briefly in the text in the next chapter.

2. Drawing on the concept of globalisation also opens up a can of worms about the status of this concept, and in particular the ways in which it can conflate explanation and description, and end up with the tautology that globalisation is caused by globalisation (see Rosenberg 2000, 2005; also Axford 2013). While I accept that this critique is true of globalisation insofar as it claims theoretical status, it is not true insofar as globalisation can usefully be related to a specific period of history within capitalism (Gamble 2014; Kiely 2014). Indeed, one might note that Rosenberg has a great deal to say about globalisation in relation to state sovereignty, but far less to say about globalisation in relation to capitalism, a strange omission for a Marxist. Globalisation is discussed further in later chapters, and in particular in Chap. 3.
3. This book does not, however, attempt to discuss in any detail the question of hegemony in the international order. On hegemony, see the valuable contribution of Worth (2014).
4. The term "marxian" is deliberately used here to emphasise how this work, like Panitch and Gindin, draws on the Marxist tradition in a selective way, but in ways which do not satisfy many "Marxists" of various persuasions. Like Panitch and Gindin (2012), this book draws on the Marxist tradition but not in such a way to defend some idea of Marxism as the only body of thought worth defending or engaging. Still less does it mean that engagement should only be with contemporary Marxists.

## References


Arrighi, G. 2007. *Adam Smith in Beijing*. London: Verso.

Axford, B. 2013. *Theories of Globalization*. Cambridge: Polity.

Barnett, T. 2004. *The Pentagon's New Map*. Berkley: Berkley Publishing Group.

Beckley, M. 2011/2012. China's Century? *International Security* 36(3): 41–78.

Frank, A.G. 1969. *Capitalism and Underdevelopment in Latin America*. New York: Monthly Review Press.

Frank, A.G. 1998. *Re-Orient*. Berkeley: University of California Press.

Gamble, A. 2014. *Crisis without End?* Basingstoke: Palgrave.

Hobson, J. 2004. *The Eastern Origins of Western Civilisation*. Cambridge: Cambridge University Press.

Ikenberry, G.J. 2014. The Logic of Order: Westphalia, Liberalism and the Evolution of International Order in the Modern Era. In *Power, Order and Change in World Politics*, ed. G.J. Ikenberry, 83–106. Cambridge: Cambridge University Press.

Kiely, R. 2010. *Rethinking Imperialism*. Basingstoke: Palgrave.
Kiely, R. 2014. Imperialism or Globalization?…Or Imperialism *and* Globalization: Theorizing the International after Rosenberg's 'Post-Mortem'. *Journal of International Relations and Development* 17(2): 274–300.
Kiely, R. 2015. *The BRICs, US 'Decline' and Global Transformations*. London: Palgrave.
Nye, J. 2015. *Is the American Century Over?* Cambridge: Polity.
Panitch, L., and S. Gindin. 2012. *The Making of Global Capitalism*. London: Verso.
Pomeranz, K. 2001. *The Great Divergence: China, Europe and the Making of the Modern World Economy*. Princeton: Princeton University Press.
Rosenberg, J. 2000. *The Follies of Globalisation Theory*. London: Verso.
Rosenberg, J. 2005. Globalization Theory: A Postmortem. *International Politics* 42(1): 2–74.
Saull, R. 2012. Rethinking Hegemony: Uneven Development, Historical Blocs and the World Economic Crisis. *International Studies Quarterly* 56(2): 323–338.
Wallerstein, I. 1974. *The Modern World System*, vol. 1. New York: Academic Press.
Worth, O. 2014. *Rethinking Hegemony*. Basingstoke: Palgrave.

CHAPTER 2

# The "Rise of the South" and International Relations and Development Theory

**Abstract** This chapter introduces the argument that the South has risen in recent years. It outlines two initial arguments: (1) that there has been a rise and this is a threat to the USA and the West; (2) that there has been a rise and this is because of market friendly policies as advocated by the West. It then relates these views to international relations (IR) theory—showing how realists and liberal internationalists respond to these questions—and shows that while these approaches are different, they are not objective, but in many respects "recommendations" for how the USA should respond to these changes. It then introduces approaches more critical of US hegemony (world systems theory [WST], global history and dependency theory), and in doing so shows how these are also perspectives on development. The chapter then moves on to explicitly consider the development question, showing how older modernisation theory overlaps, despite their considerable differences, with contemporary neoliberalism, in that both see contact with "the West" as desirable and progressive. And in particular I show how liberal internationalism and neoliberal political economy can be seen as new versions of modernisation theory. The chapter then focuses in more depth on dependency theory, arguing that, for all its problems, this approach does address important questions about inequality, marginalisation and subordination in the international order. The chapter then suggests that we might think of the rise (and fall) of the South in terms of modernisation and dependency *approaches* (rather than the specific details of these problematic theories), albeit updated to



R. Kiely, *The Rise and Fall of Emerging Powers*,
DOI 10.1007/978-3-319-34012-8_2

take account of new realities (including the uneven and unequal effects of China's rise and premature industrialisation in much of the rest of the South). The final section provides an initial introduction to the rise and fall of the South through the lens of these two broad approaches.

**Keywords** Development theory • International relations theory • Realism • Liberal internationalism • World systems theory • Modernisation • Dependency

This chapter introduces the argument that the South has risen in recent years. It shows that there are two broad arguments around this: (1) there has been a rise and this is a threat to the USA and the West; (2) there has been a rise and this is because of market friendly policies as advocated by the West. The chapter first briefly outlines the rise, and then relates this to the most influential "mainstream" theories of international relations (IR), realism and liberal internationalism. The chapter will not provide a detailed exposition of these theories and will instead focus on how realists and liberal internationalists respond to the question of the South's alleged rise. It will show that while these approaches are different, in many respects the theories are interesting less as analyses of the international order, and more in terms of the "recommendations" they make for how the USA should respond to these changes. In other words, these can in many respects be considered theories about the sources of and threats to US leadership of the international order. This is perhaps most obvious from the fact that there is very little work which examines the perspectives of, say, Chinese realists or liberal internationalists. We might therefore ask who IR theory is for (Cox 1981), and this question is used to then explore more critical approaches, and specifically world systems, dependency and "new global histories" approaches. In introducing these perspectives, the link between IR and development theory will then be made, and the chapter will examine the two main "grand theories" of development which were influential from the 1950s through to the 1970s: modernisation and dependency theory. While these two approaches are now considered out of date, and in some respects rightly so, I will go on to suggest that they retain some utility for understanding both the contemporary international order and the related question of development. In briefly discussing neoliberalism and its understanding of development, I will suggest that liberal internationalism and neoliberal political economy can be seen as new versions of modernisation theory, and that much of the rise of emerging markets discourse implicitly draws on these understandings of international order and development. At the same time, those who argue—as this book does—that both international order and development can be usefully analysed in terms of the existence of cores and peripheries (even if the mechanisms need to be clarified) draw in part from some of the claims of world systems and dependency approaches. It will become clear in what follows that this does not necessarily mean adherence to these theories (and, indeed, it will be argued that dependency cannot even be regarded as a theory), but the wider book will show how the uneven development of global capitalism can give rise to cores and peripheries, and the rise of the South has not changed this.

The chapter therefore has four main sections. First, it provides a brief introduction to the idea of the rise of the South. Second, it provides a brief introduction to theories of IR and specifically focuses on what these theories have to say about the rise of the South. Third, it provides an introduction to theories of development and how these might be used to explain the rise of the South. In bringing these sections together, I will simplify somewhat, and try to think about the rise of the South in terms of modernisation and dependency approaches. It will be clear from the discussion that follows that there are problems with these approaches, and what this chapter tries to establish, along with the rest of the book, is that we might usefully think of the rise (and fall) of the South through a dialogue with these approaches, rather than through rigid adherence to the claims of these (highly problematic) theories. The fourth section makes some tentative attempts to apply the approaches discussed to the rise of the BRICs, with specific attention paid to the period before 2008.

## Rise of the South, Decline of the USA: An Introduction

The decade of the 2000s and beyond is often seen as the time of the inexorable rise of the South, led by a group of large developing countries sometimes known as the BRICs (O' Neill 2001; OECD 2010a, b; UNDP 2013). This rise reflected high growth rates, increased foreign investment to and from the South, and increased trade between countries of the South. The size of the BRICs meant that there were positive spin-offs for the rest of the South, with various acronyms such as N-11 and MINT (Mexico, Indonesia, Nigeria and Turkey) used to describe those rapidly growing countries seemingly destined to follow in the footsteps of the BRICs (O'Neill et al. 2005: 12; O' Neill 2013: 232–5; 2014). Moreover, the global financial crisis seemingly intensified these processes, as recovery in the South from 2010 onwards was rapid (Goldman Sachs 2010). Growing demand from the BRICs could lead a global recovery, part of which entailed a wider delinking of the South from dependence on the global North, as "business cycles in emerging markets have gradually *decoupled* from those in advanced economies, as trade diversification, commodity strength and, particularly, the emergence of China took over the G7 as the main global factor behind fluctuations in the emerging world" (Yeyati and Williams 2012: 17).

There is plenty of evidence to back these claims. Tables 2.1 and 2.2 show the rates of growth of the BRICs (up to and including 2010, the year of substantial recovery from the crisis), and of developed and developing countries both before and after the crisis, and they show considerably higher rates of growth in the South than in the North. There has also been a decline in North–North trade as a proportion of total international trade, an increase in the proportion of exports originating from the developing world (from 23% in 1990 to 37% by 2008), and an increase in the proportion accounted for by South–South trade, which rose from 7.8% in 1990 to 19% by 2008 (OECD 2010a: 71). Total direct foreign investment increased from $59 billion in 1982 to $1.45 trillion by 2013, while

**Table 2.1** Annual average real GDP growth rates (*source*—UNCTAD 2015c: Handbook of Statistics)

| | *1980–1990* | *1990–2000* | *2000–2005* | *2006* | *2007* | *2008* | *2009* | *2010* |
|---|---|---|---|---|---|---|---|---|
| Brazil | 2.8 | 2.9 | 2.8 | 3.7 | 5.7 | 5.1 | −0.2 | 7.5 |
| China | 10.3 | 10.4 | 9.6 | 11.6 | 13 | 9 | 8.7 | 10.3 |
| India | 5.8 | 6 | 6.9 | 9.8 | 9.3 | 7.3 | 7.4 | 10.4 |
| Russia | N.A. | −4.7 | 6.2 | 7.4 | 8.1 | 5.6 | −7.9 | 4.8 |

**Table 2.2** World output growth (annual percentage change) (*source*: UNCTAD 2014a: 2; 2015a: 1)

| | *2006* | *2007* | *2008* | *2009* | *2010* | *2011* | *2012* | *2013* | *2014* |
|---|---|---|---|---|---|---|---|---|---|
| World | 4.1 | 4 | 1.5 | −2.1 | 4.1 | 2.8 | 2.2 | 2.4 | 2.5 |
| Developed world | 2.8 | 2.5 | 0 | −3.7 | 2.6 | 1.4 | 1.1 | 1.3 | 1.6 |
| Developing world | 7.7 | 8.0 | 2.6 | 2.6 | 7.8 | 6.0 | 4.7 | 4.8 | 4.5 |

developing countries increased their share of world production from 25% to 47% from 1980 to 2010 (UNCTAD 2013: 3; 2014b: 2). In the period after 1992, there was a massive boom in foreign investment. For much of this period around two-thirds of foreign direct investment (FDI) went to developed countries and one-third to developing (and transition) economies, but, by 2012, developing and transition economies accounted for 52% of global FDI inflows, by 2013 the percentage was 54% and by 2015 it was 55% (UNCTAD 2013: 2; 2014b: 2; 2015b: 2). Thus in 2013, of the \$1.45 trillion total FDI, developing economies received \$778 billion and in 2014 (when total FDI fell) the figure was \$681 billion, compared to \$499 billion for developed countries (UNCTAD 2014b: 2; 2015b: 2, 3). The BRICS were central to this change in foreign investment shares, with (in 2013) China the second largest recipient (and Hong Kong China fourth), Russia third, Brazil fifth and India fourteenth (UNCTAD 2014b: 4). Furthermore, the BRICS (including South Africa) have also emerged as major foreign investors themselves, and in 2013, outward FDI flows from developing countries stood at 32.2% of the total outflows (of \$1.41 trillion), in contrast to 1998 when the proportion (of a much lower figure) was just 7% (UNCTAD 2014b: 5), although the share is still dominated by China (and Hong Kong, China) and Russia (UNCTAD 2014b: 7). Thus, the OECD (2010a: 5, 16) states that:

> The new millennium saw the resumption...of a trend towards strong convergence in per capita income with the high income countries. The number of...countries doubling the average per capita growth of the high income OECD countries...more than quintupled during this period (from 12 to 65), and the number of poor countries more than halved (from 55 to 25)... Latin America's per capita growth rates were the highest since 1965–70...In Africa...GDP growth for the region averaged 4.4% between 2000 and 2007.

While we might talk about the rise of the BRICs and of the South, above all there is China. At market prices, China's contribution to global GDP was 1.6% in 1990, but by 2008 it stood at 7.1% (Nolan 2012: 1). It has the largest amount of foreign exchange reserves in the world—\$3197 billion in June 2011, more than double the amount of Japan, the second country (Nolan 2012: 4). Its exports grew by 14% per annum in the 1990s and by 25% in the 2000s (Nolan 2012: 4), and by 2009 it was the world's largest exporter (Nolan 2012: 55). It is a major foreign holder of US public debt and at May 2013, it held 23.2% of the total foreign holdings of US government debt, compared to 19.6% for Japan, the next major foreign holder (US Treasury Department 2013). In the period from 2000 to 2014, the annual US trade deficit with China increased from $83 billion to $342 billion (US Census Bureau 2015). In 2006, possibly as much as one-third of the US current account deficit was accounted for by Chinese manufacturing imports (Hung 2016: 126–7). Speaking in 2012, Gerard Lyons, chief economist at Standard Chartered Bank, "the three most important words in the past decade were not the 'war on terror' but 'made in China.' On present trends, the three most important words of this decade will be 'owned by China'" (Financial Times 2011: 9). This is not to say that the rise of the South is reducible to China's rise, but at the same time the supposed rise of the South would not have happened without it.

According to the OECD (2010a: 15), these developments are indicative of a transformation in the international order, in which "the world's economic centre of gravity has moved towards the east and south, from OECD members to emerging economies ... This realignment of the world economy ... represents a structural change of historical significance." In other words, we are witnessing a transformation of the international order based on "the rise of the East," above all India and especially China (OECD 2010a: 37, 44), and this in turn is facilitating the rise of the South as a whole (Khanna 2009). Some writers, especially Western liberals, suggest that this will lead to mutual benefits for North and South alike (OECD 2010b: 7; O' Neill 2013), at least in terms of economic growth and increasing output, so long as appropriate policies are carried out. And these are in essence "market friendly policies," often associated with neoliberalism, which is discussed further below (World Bank 2002).

On the other hand, others suggest that this development reflects the rise of what has variously been described as the Beijing Consensus (Ramo 2004; Halper 2010), the China model (Zhao 2010), or state capitalism (Bremmer 2010; The Economist 2012), all of which challenge the US-centred, neoliberal Washington Consensus. It is also illustrated by the fact that the BRICs—an idea that originated in a Western investment bank—has now become a geopolitical reality, with annual BRIC and (with the addition of South Africa) BRICS summits (BRICS 2013) part of a more assertive "new South" in the international order (Alden et al. 2012: 92). Some see this rise as a cause for regret (Mearsheimer 2006; Kagan 2012), as China's rise points to "a most troublesome export: *the example of the China model,* " one based on "*state capitalism*, a Chinese capitalism based on "*market authoritarianism*," which gives support to dictators in the developing world (Halper 2010: 32, 10, 11, xx, 31). Gideon Rachman (2010: 39) thus refers to an axis of authoritarianism which "shares a distinctive approach to the world that contrasts sharply with liberal attitudes … A world in which authoritarian powers wield considerably more influence looks very different from the years 1991–2008, when the world order was informally based on two central facts—American power and globalization."

A further position can be discerned from those who in some respects analytically agree that state capitalism and a China model or Beijing Consensus has emerged, but who draw very different conclusions. Indeed, they welcome the rise of the BRICs precisely because they are seen as a *challenge* to Western and US hegemony (Dirlik 2006; Mahbubani 2008; Chase-Dunn 2013; Desai 2012, 2013; Escobar 2013; Subin 2014). For the late Giovanni Arrighi (2007: 9–10), the USA faces a "terminal crisis," reflected in the failures of the war on terror, US deficits and the financial crisis. This suggests then an inexorable rise of the South with China as the undisputed leader, and the possible relative decline of the USA. This challenge is welcomed because US leadership has promoted an international order which has not led to equality and mutual recognition, but is instead one based on hierarchy, exploitation and marginalisation. In some respects then, this approach is based on arguments linked to world systems and dependency theory, which are considered in more depth below.

This section then has provided a brief introduction to the rise of the South in the 2000s. It has suggested that this rise has been led by China and so China's rise—and how it has impacted on the other BRICs and the South—must be a central part of the story that follows. But from the brief quotations above, it is also clear that there are different ways of examining this rise, and specifically different ways of understanding the implications of the rise of China, the BRICs and the South. From within the West, there is an optimistic position which suggests that China and the South's rise represents an opportunity for the West, while there is a more pessimistic position which suggests that the rise of the South, at least under China's leadership, is a threat. These two positions are not necessarily mutually exclusive and one, for instance, might argue that China's rise was an economic opportunity for, but also a geopolitical threat to, "the West" and the USA in particular. But we need to know more about these arguments for—and indeed other approaches to—understanding contemporary IR. This is the task of the next section.

## The Rise of the South and IR Theory

From the brief quotations above, it is clear that some writers (such as Mearsheimer 2001) see China's rise as a threat, while others regard it as an opportunity (for the West), particularly for economic reasons (O' Neill 2013). The former thus see the rise of China and its allies as a threat to the USA and Western hegemony, while the latter largely do not. Still others accept the argument that China and the BRICs are rising, but actually welcome this challenge to US hegemony. We will examine this third perspective at the end of this section, but, first, we need to consider the first two positions.

In terms of IR theory, the first position is associated with realism and the second with liberal internationalism. There are differences of opinion among realists and among liberal internationalists, not only over specific policy issues (such as the decisions to go to war with Iraq in 2003, where there were pro-war liberal internationalists and anti-war realists), but also over wider points of theory. But at the risk of oversimplification, realists argue that the world is an imperfect one and the international order is essentially anarchic.[1] What this means is that there is no overall global leviathan to maintain order between the basic components of the international order, which are in essence nation-states. The international order is therefore one prone to conflict, and realism is a theory which attempts to analyse the ways in which order can, to some degree, be maintained in the context of anarchy. There is disagreement over the extent to which an aggressive national interest must be pursued in the name of security, as against those defensive realists who advocate more pragmatic responses (on China, compare Mearsheimer 2001; Kirshner 2010). But all realists share the view that the international order is based on anarchy and that nation-states are the central players in this system.

It is therefore not surprising that an offensive realist like Mearsheimer argues that the rise of China is one that is likely to lead to conflict in the international order, as one hegemonic challenger is considered a threat by the current hegemonic power. Thus as early as 2001, Mearsheimer (2001: 401–2) argued that "it is not too late for the United States to reverse course and do what it can to slow the rise of China. In fact the structural imperatives of the international system, which are powerful, will probably force the United States to abandon its policy of constructive engagement in the near future." This is not surprising because China "will become an aggressive state determined to achieve regional hegemony" (Mearsheimer

2001: 402). The conservative Stefan Halper highlights the threat to liberal hegemony presented by the rise of "market authoritarianism" and the idea that China is a model for the rest of the South, and therefore a threat to Western hegemony, and more specifically the US-led Washington Consensus. Paralleling the arguments of Halper, Rotberg (2008: viii) has described China's "extractive and exploitive" new scramble for Africa, while Navarro (2007: 100) argues that China's amoral involvement in Africa is "a threat that will colonise and economically enslave the vast majority of the continent's population." Much is made, like Halper (2010: 11), of China's support for authoritarian regimes as well as China's self-interest in extracting resources from the region (Cooper 2003). Such negative characterisations are contrasted with progressive Western intervention, concerned with development, human rights and poverty reduction (Council on Foreign Relations 2006).

In contrast, the likes of the Organisation for Economic Cooperation and Development (OECD) and Jim O' Neill are far more sanguine about the rise of both China and the South, arguing that it constitutes an opportunity for the West. This argument in part reflects their particular focus—which is also the main focus of this book—which is one that focuses on political economy, or perhaps even just orthodox economics (which is *not* the main focus of this book!). But one of their arguments implies that opportunity exists because it is in effect leading to economic interdependence. And it is this idea of interdependence which is central to a different understanding of international order, associated with liberal internationalism. Keohane and Nye (1977: 7) most famously defined interdependence as "mutual dependence. Interdependence in world politics refers to situations characterised by reciprocal effects among countries." Moravcsik (1997: 520) similarly argues that "each state seeks to realize its distinctive preferences under varying conditions imposed by the preferences of other states." He further argues that:

> Liberal international relations theory rests on a "bottom up" or pluralist view of politics. Functionally differentiated individuals and groups define material and ideational goals independently of politics, then seek to advance those ends through political means. Social actors favour some economic, social, cultural and domestic political arrangements rather than others—that is, particular structures of economic production and exchange, social relations, cultural practice, or domestic political rule. For the purpose of studying world politics, the critical source of social interest is globalisation—that is, the changing opportunities and incentives to engage in transnational economic, social and cultural activity. (Moravcsik 2008: 236)

Specifically applied to the rise of China and of the South, a liberal internationalist position argues that this is not necessarily a threat to US hegemony. In particular, the argument is made that US hegemony is based on a specific kind of leadership, which attempts to integrate other countries into transactions based on positive-sum games, in which all states benefit from participation. The USA has in effect constructed a system of hegemony which rests on the active participation and consensus of other states. If it is an "empire" it is one based on "Empire by integration" (Lundestad 1998). This means that "(w)hen a liberal state is hegemonic, the subordinate actors in a system have a variety of channels and mechanisms for registering their interests with the hegemon. Transnational relations are the vehicles by which subordinate actors in the system represent their interest to the hegemonic power and the vehicle through which consensus between the hegemon and the lesser powers is achieved" (Deudney and Ikenberry 1999: 185).

In terms of China and the USA then, for Ikenberry (2008: 23), "China does not just face the United States; it faces a Western-centred system that is open, integrated and rule based, with wide and deep political foundations. The nuclear revolution, meanwhile, has made war among great powers unlikely—eliminating the major tool that rising powers have used to overturn international systems defended by declining hegemonic states. Today's Western order, in short, is hard to overturn and easy to join."

Important then for liberals is the fact China cooperates because it has gained from membership of the liberal international order. It has joined the World Trade Organisation, is now a permanent member of the UN Security Council, and, most relevant for our purposes, is heavily integrated into global circuits of capital through foreign investment flows (both to and from China), international trade and the purchase of US debt. While there remain areas of difficulty, particularly over the nature of China's political system, the question of Taiwan, and sovereignty in the South China Sea, growing economic cooperation is more significant in the long term. The Obama administration's Asia Pivot policy from 2012 onwards is also seen in this light, for it is regarded by liberals as an attempt to further integrate the region into the liberal international order. On the other hand, realism tends to emphasise alleged US decline, rising Chinese economic and military power, and the reality of those conflicts over Taiwan and in the South China Sea, and cases of intervention led by the USA elsewhere in the developing world, which are generally opposed by China.

This is not the place for a full analysis of these issues, though they are taken up again quite briefly in the final section below. What I want to do here instead is emphasise one further point, which is more relevant to our discussion. I have already suggested that it would be a mistake to think that there is only one realist and one liberal position on these questions. Realists are far from united in viewing China's rise as a threat and liberal internationalists may take more aggressive attitudes towards China given that it is not a liberal democratic power. But there is something even more significant to say at this point, which is that, despite their differences, realists and liberal internationalists might actually share a number of assumptions. First, as already suggested, it is perfectly possible to promote a liberal internationalist position in terms of political economy while taking a more realist position in terms of geopolitics. Second, and more significant for our purposes, what is particularly significant is that the realists and liberals that we have briefly cited all agree that the USA is the hegemonic power, and that in some respects it is the *legitimate hegemonic power*. What much of the IR debate on the rise of the South is actually about is how "we," that is the USA and its Western allies, might and indeed *should* respond to the rise of China, the BRICs and their supposed allies (Kirshner 2010). This is particularly interesting for realism, because it claims to be a theory which is analytical but not normative—in other words, it analyses power in the international order without taking a moral stand on it. But if this is the case, then why does Mearsheimer (2001: 11–12) argue that "offensive realism is mainly a descriptive theory ... but it is also a prescriptive theory. States *should* behave according to dictates of offensive realism, because it outlines the best way to survive in a dangerous world." On the face of it, this is not an apology for American power because it is a prescription that could be applied to all states. But if applied to all states, it is a weak analysis because Mearsheimer conflates *being* a hegemonic power with *challenging to be* a hegemonic power, and these are not one and the same thing. Indeed, being a hegemonic challenger carries all sorts of risks and, in fact, "survival is the number one goal of great powers" (Mearsheimer 2001: 46). If this is the case then accommodation to an existing hegemonic power might be the best goal for any rational state, and Mearsheimer (2001: 30) stresses that "great powers are rational actors." But more specifically, what Mearsheimer is arguing is that the USA *should* take action to ensure that it remains the leading power in the international order, and, in normative terms, this cannot help but be an apology for US hegemony. Halper (above) is even more explicit in his contrast between desirable US hegemony and the undesirable threat from China. Put another way, while we hear much about realism, in effect what this usually means is *US realism* as opposed to, say, Chinese or Brazilian realism. This is not to deny the existence of Chinese or Brazilian realism in IR, but it is to deny the notion that realism is value free. Within China, there are those that believe that the promotion of China's national interest might lead to some form of conflict with the USA, but the more prominent view is that China's rise will largely be on the basis of engagement and cooperation with the West, through "peace and development" as opposed to the "war and revolution" of the Maoist era (Zhu 2010; also Foot 2006). But more relevant for our purposes, it appears that US realism might not be so different from liberalism precisely because the USA has exercised its power through a liberal international order, in contrast to previous hegemonic powers. But if this is the case, then realists cannot simply discuss the rise and fall of hegemonic powers as if it was a purely cyclical process, because the sources of hegemony might vary across time and place. In particular, as will become clear in Chaps. 3 and 4, focusing on national shares of GDP, or trade deficits or national debt levels, not least with China, might be misleading measures of leadership within the context of the USA' specifically liberal and interdependent sources of hegemony.

What this rather brief discussion suggests then, is that we need to be more self-reflective on the question of not only what, but who, IR theory is for (Cox 1981). And this points leads us to consider a number of theories and approaches which are far more questioning of US hegemony. These might include various critical theories such as world systems theories, dependency theory, post-colonial theory and theories of "new global histories." Immanuel Wallerstein's world systems theory (WST) argues that capitalism should be theorised as a single world capitalist economy, based on the "full development of market trade" (Wallerstein 1974: 391) as emerged from the sixteenth century onwards. The increased spread of market relations gave rise to a global division of labour and specialisation, in which different components of the world system sold goods on the international market. Through specialisation came differentiation, with some parts of the world having a monopoly over other parts, and therefore gaining a greater share of global wealth. Wallerstein characterises this division as a three-tiered one: a core, periphery and semi-periphery. A pattern of labour control arises in response to different forms of economic activity, with the core using wage labour, the semi-periphery using sharecropping and the periphery using coerced cash crop labour. This division is reinforced by the development of varying state structures, with strong states developing in the core, and weak states in the periphery. What is most important for our purposes is Wallerstein's three-tier division of the world into core, semi-periphery and periphery, and in the post-1945 era, Wallerstein suggests that a new semi-periphery has developed in southern Europe and East Asia, which acts as a buffer between core and periphery. Underdevelopment theory (UDT), which can be considered one variant of dependency theory, argued along similar lines, suggesting that the world is divided into metropoles or cores, and satellites or peripheries, and that that the former develop by underdeveloping the latter. Thus, development and underdevelopment are two sides of the same coin—the poor world is poor because it has been underdeveloped by the developed world, and the rich world is rich because it has underdeveloped the poor world, which "remain underdeveloped for the lack of access to their own surplus" (Frank 1969: 9). Therefore, some nations develop at the expense of others in a zero-sum game. Capitalism therefore needs to be conceptualised as a world system, divided between exploiting metropoles and exploited satellites.

In this way, IR is conceptualised as an order based on *hierarchy* rather than anarchy or interdependence. Crucially, this hierarchy is not one that exists only within states, but also between states, regions and different locations, as is captured by the idea of core, semi-periphery and periphery. This argument places development at the centre of understanding IR, and we consider this in depth in a moment. But before doing so, we should briefly consider the fate of at least some version of WST and dependency theory in the light of changes in the international order from the 1970 onwards. For what was problematic about these approaches was that they tended to suggest that developing countries would remain statically underdeveloped so long as they remained part of the Western-dominated order. But clearly this was not the case in the 1970s, at least for some developing countries, and above all the East Asian newly industrialising countries such as South Korea and Taiwan. While it is certainly true that such countries did not simply embrace the world economy along the lines suggested by neoliberals (see Lal 1984), it is also true that they did not rapidly industrialise without some forms of engagement with the Western-dominated world economy, and, above all, through processes of export promotion, accompanied by state direction and protection (Amsden 1989; Wade 1990; Evans 1995; Kohli 2004). Both dependency (or at least UDT) and WST had to come to terms with these changes, much as they might have to also account for more recent changes associated with the rise of the BRICs and the rising South discourse. Wallerstein's division into three zones, and use of the concept of semi-periphery, may help in terms of *description*, but in accounting for the shift of parts of East Asia from periphery to semi-periphery (or BRIC countries from semi-periphery to core), it is somewhat light on *explanation*. What is significant is the shift in the agenda of WST, and the effective abandonment of the claims of UDT (and, we will see, the more problematic abandonment of the concept of dependency). In particular the former has shifted its focus to an understanding of the rise and fall of hegemonic powers, in which the demise of US hegemony is a recurring theme (Wallerstein 2003). Thus, although critical of much work of earlier WST and his own UDT, Frank's later work (1998: 26–34, 46) can be located within a newer tradition of "global history" (Bin Wong 1997; Pomeranz 2001), much of which takes an analysis of the world system as its point of departure. Frank argues that the world system has historically been centred on Asia, and that Europe became the dominant power only in the nineteenth century. Frank (1998: 75) argues that the period from 1400 to 1800 was one characterised by an Asian-dominated world economy, and that Europe remained a marginal player in this order. Central to this claim is the fact that Europe had a long-standing trade deficit with Asia, and that Europe financed this by plundering of gold from the Americas, which financed the import of goods from Asia. He also claims that Asia as late as 1800 was a more efficient economic producer than Europe (Frank 1998: 172–4). Europe gradually overtook Asia as the latter went into economic crisis from 1750 onwards. Central to Frank's argument is the idea that the West as the centre of the international order is historically unusual and indeed is coming to an end. Giovanni Arrighi (2007) also makes this case, and suggests that from the 1950s, the Western capital and energy-intensive path of industrial development reached its limits, and the East Asian labour-intensive and energy saving "industrious revolution" began to challenge Western hegemony and restore Asia's position as the central region in the world economy. While much of the South suffered from the debt crisis of the 1980s, East Asia continued its resurgence and it is this region which is set to challenge US hegemony, a decline further eroded by the military adventurism of the Bush II administration from 2001 to 2008 and (we might add) the global financial crisis.

More specifically, those who welcome the China challenge contrast China's aid "without conditions" to the Western imposition of power. Human rights discourses are used selectively, as is so-called humanitarian intervention, often with negative and violent consequences (Chomsky 2002; Chandler 2005). Good governance and market friendly intervention are criticised for their failure to secure the conditions for successful development in the continent, and instead involve a set of policies which integrate these countries into the world economy in a subordinate and dependent way, thus reinforcing Western domination (Chang 2007; Kiely 2010). China's rise thus represents a challenge to Western hegemony and indeed imperialism (Escobar 2013; Subin 2014). Both sides of this debate therefore see the rise of China as a new leader of the South as a fact, and the differences are over whether or not this is a desirable occurrence.[2] The debate here then is over whether at least one of the following is something to be welcomed or not: the rise of the BRICs; the China model; market authoritarianism; state capitalism; the Beijing Consensus; the challenge to a liberal international order; the challenge to the neoliberal (post-) Washington Consensus.

However, it is far from clear that these things are as established as is sometimes assumed, and the rise of China and the new South actually needs to be put into context. First, the Chinese Communist Party is itself sceptical of terms like the Beijing Consensus (Kennedy 2010; Breslin 2011) and it is hard to clearly identify a single China model within China, let alone overseas (Hameiri and Jones 2016; Mulvad 2015). While China itself might be regarded as in some sense a state capitalist country (Bremmer 2010), this is hardly a "model" exclusive to China (Knight 2014; Breslin 2011; Chang 2002; Wade 1990; Amsden 1989; Kohli 2004; Fine and Saraswati 2013). In terms of aid to the South, insofar as we have reliable figures, it appears that Africa received around \$35 billion in Chinese concessional loans for construction projects from 2000 to 2014, mainly through the Forum on China–Africa Cooperation, or FOCAC (Lee 2014: 41; Taylor 2014). Although the precise nature of this aid is not well known, Lee (2014: 41) suggests that the \$2 billion that went to Zambia in this period was subject to a higher rate of interest than World Bank loans (2% against 1.7%), had a smaller grant element (23% against 35%), and a shorter repayment period (10–15 against 15–25 years). These concessional loans were also conditional on non-competitive sourcing from Chinese companies. In terms of investment, in copper mines in Zambia Chinese companies tend to draw on lower wages and often have poor working conditions, though in keeping with a "long-termist" state capitalist policy, they are also less likely to lay off workers than Western companies, as in the copper price fall in the immediate aftermath of the 2008 financial crisis (Lee 2014: 61).[3]

These perspectives then essentially challenge the implicit Western or indeed American-centrism of IR theory. These are theories which claim to be perspectives for the South. But perhaps what is most interesting is that they too essentially uphold the argument that the South is rising, for these perspectives have moved from an excessive pessimism which argued that the South cannot develop so long as it remains part of the Western-dominated international order, to one which suggests that, under China's leadership, the South has developed rapidly and is indeed moving to a position whereby it can at some point challenge that Western hegemony, and this is something to be welcomed. One might say that perhaps this view has moved from an excessive pessimism to an excessive optimism (with some wishful thinking added into the mix). But what should be clear from this discussion is that we have clearly moved to an analysis of the international order in which development takes a central place. We therefore need to consider this question, and how it relates to IR, and we do so in the next section.

## The Rise of the South and Development Theory

Although these predated 1945, the post-war international order saw an intensification of debates in US IR over liberal internationalism and realism. Running parallel to these debates, development theory emerged as a body of thought in its own right. Compatible with both realism and liberal internationalism, modernisation theory emerged as the dominant paradigm for understanding development in what came to be called the third world. This theory was not of course isolated from the Cold War, and both superpowers supported political independence for the colonies, though both of course were concerned that they exercise considerable influence over the political trajectory of the newly independent sovereign states. Modernisation theory essentially claimed that developing societies were backward and undeveloped, and therefore in need of development. Walt Rostow (1960) most famously argued that all nation-states pass through similar stages of development, so that poorer societies in the 1960s were at a similar stage of development to, say, Britain in the 1780s. The task of development was to hasten the transition to development in the poorer societies. Rostow argued that this was good for developing societies, as they would become richer, but also for the security of the West, as richer societies were less likely to be attracted by the communist alternative (see also Huntington 1968). Modernisation theory suggested that the task of development could be facilitated by poorer countries embracing Western investment, technology and values such as entrepreneurship and meritocracy.

For our purposes then, what was significant about modernisation theory was its recommendation that the developing world embrace the West as the basis for development. This embrace might mean adopting Western policies (and in the post-war era this did not mean neoliberal policies), but, more crucially, becoming significant actors in the liberal international order. There was enough *reapolitik* in modernisation theory to accept that liberal democracy might not be possible in the short term, and indeed authoritarianism might be a useful counter to the Communist "threat" (Huntington 1968). But the argument was one that suggested Western investment, growth, technology and cultural values would allow a process of modernisation which would ensure that countries remained part of the liberal capitalist world (Rostow 1960).

Modernisation theory also championed the idea that industrialisation was necessary for progress and development to take place, an idea that in some respects cut across the political and ideological divide (Kitching 1982). Thus, some structuralist economists made the case for industrialisation precisely on the grounds that, in some respects, integration into the liberal capitalist economy was problematic. In particular, one of the legacies of colonialism was that third world countries specialised in producing primary products, and this led to an excessive dependence on the world price movements of the one or two goods that accounted for most of their foreign exchange earnings. This was in contrast to the developed countries, which were far more industrialised and diversified, and so were not excessively reliant on the price movements of a handful of products. Moreover, Raul Prebisch (1959) and Hans Singer (1950) argued that primary producers faced certain disadvantages which meant that there was a tendency for the terms of trade to decline for primary goods as against industrial goods. Prebisch and Singer suggested that this tendency occurred because there was a low income elasticity of demand for primary products; in other words, as average incomes rise, so consumers spend a disproportionate amount of their income on primary products. Furthermore, while the prices of manufactured goods may fall, they are less likely to fall as quickly as those of primary goods as there were many primary goods producers but comparatively few producers of industrial goods. Clearly then, and in sharp contrast to modernisation theory, this account of inequality focused on hierarchies in the world economy, and how colonial powers (or powerful agrarian landowners) had enforced specialisation in lower-value primary production in the colonies. But at the same time, like modernisation theory, this account suggested that development in the third world could be achieved through pro-industrialisation policies designed to overcome the colonial legacy. In this way, poorer countries could reduce their dependence on the import of expensive manufactures and the export of cheap primary goods. This policy of import substitution industrialisation (ISI) was the main development strategy employed in the third world from the 1950s (or earlier) until the late 1970s and early 1980s.

In contrast to modernisation theory, an alternative more critical view emerged which challenged the idea that development was a linear process of catch-up by poor countries with rich countries. Like the structuralism of Prebisch and Singer, this approach emphasised hierarchies in the international order, but also suggested that industrialisation did not so much alleviate as in some respects intensify this problem. This was the basic starting point for dependency theory. The mechanisms that sustained dependence included reliance on foreign capital, foreign technology and foreign markets. Furthermore, the industrialisation that was said to be occurring in the developing world was highly exploitative and reliant on cheap labour. None of this was leading to convergence with the developed world; instead, it was simply promoting new forms of subordination, hierarchy and dependence in the world economy. As we have already seen, in the guise of UDT, dependency was reduced to a crude zero-sum game which suggested that the rich world was rich only because it had underdeveloped the poor world, implying that protectionist ISI policies did not go far enough, and that delinking from the Western-dominated world economy was the only effective way forward for the third world (Frank 1969). But more flexible accounts of dependency suggested that concrete manifestations of dependence did not mean stagnation or static underdevelopment, but it did mean the emergence of forms of development which diverged sharply from earlier periods of capitalism.

This was essentially what was at stake in the development for much of the period from the 1940s into the 1970s. On the one side was modernisation theory: poorer countries should embrace the opportunities provided by the Western-dominated world economy, and in the process hasten the transition to development. On the other side was dependency theory: poorer countries are poor in part because they are in a structurally subordinate and dependent position in the world economy, and thus need to find ways to protect themselves from the constraints that these hierarchies generate. In many respects this debate was and is hugely problematic. Both theories tended to overgeneralise, and make sweeping claims that saw either development (modernisation theory) or stagnation (dependency theory) as inevitable. So, while the rise of East Asian newly industrialising countries such as South Korea and Taiwan undermined crude versions of dependency theory, as these countries grew rapidly and exported to the Western economies, it is also true that these countries did not simply embrace "the West," and protected certain sectors from foreign competition in order to develop their own national industries. While this might in some respects have been compatible with modernisation theory (as opposed to neoliberalism), it was far from clear that these countries converged with the West in any simple way, and they certainly retained elements of cultural and social specificity. Moreover, the success of these countries may have rested on certain contingent factors that could not easily be replicated elsewhere. It was precisely this focus on contingency and specificity that was missing in the modernisation versus dependency theory debate (Booth 1985).

Perhaps more importantly, changes in the global economy led to important changes in the context in which development took place in the so-called periphery. The 1982 debt crisis led to a shift from ISI towards neoliberal policies that encouraged trade and investment liberalisation, privatisation, and a change in the forms of state intervention so that states in some respects came to resemble markets, in terms of internal competition, audits and partnerships with the private sector. Neoliberalism justified this shift on the grounds that ISI encouraged the promotion and protection of inefficient industries, rather than facilitating specialisation in those sectors where countries were (relatively) most competitive; in other words, it meant the promotion of the principle of comparative advantage. This was reinforced by the end of the Cold War, and the growing liberalisation of financial flows, as well as trade and investment flows, from the 1980s onwards. While in the short term, the results of neoliberal policies were disastrous, and living standards for many fell in the 1980s, the 1990s saw a new period of optimism concerning the relationship between development and globalisation, culminating in the rising South thesis in the 2000s.

What should be clear though is that this debate was essentially one about development prospects in the context of a US-led liberal international order. In one respect this debate had ended, as modernisation theory and (some) dependency theory suffered from overgeneralisation and the debate over development moved on to questions of relations between states and markets. But, oversimplifications and generalisations notwithstanding, one can see elements of the old development debate in a number of assumptions about the political economy of globalisation. This is considered in more depth in Chap. 3, but briefly it could be argued that much of the debate over poverty reduction and globalisation (World Bank 2002; Dollar and Kraay 2002) replicates some of the earlier development debate. For example, the World Bank (2002) claims that the most globalised developing countries are those that have been most successful in terms of economic growth and poverty reduction. Now this of course is not identical to the specific claims of, say, Walt Rostow, and indeed neoliberals have historically been critical of modernisation theory. But, on the other hand, the basic contention of modernisation theory—which is that developing countries should in some respects embrace the Western-dominated liberal international order—is repeated. In this understanding of the term, globalisation essentially becomes modernisation for neoliberal times (see Giddens 2000; for a critique, see Kiely 2007). And most important for our purposes, this is an argument that has been made to explain the rise of the BRICs (O' Neill 2013).

So far, the critical responses that we have focused on have regarded the South as doomed to stagnation, or, more recently, that under Chinese leadership Western hegemony is being challenged. But we also saw that some of these critical approaches suggested that the world is made up of cores and peripheries. Though it should be clear that much of the world systems approach conceptualised this division in functionalist terms, so that the core simply exploited the periphery, the latter of which simply served the functional needs of the former. Given the rise of the East Asian newly industrializing countries (NICs), and more recently the BRICs, it is not surprising that such an approach was challenged, and indeed much WST analysis shifted its focus to understanding the fall of the USA and the rise of Asia. But what if—descriptively at least—the idea of core and periphery can still be useful, even in the context of the rise of the BRICs? Such an approach might accept that all countries in the world order do in some respects "develop," but this development does not necessarily lead to convergence, catch-up, or even transformation of the international order. In particular, following earlier periods of capitalist development after 1945, we might accept two critical points: first, while capitalist development has occurred in the developing world, and most significantly in the BRICS in recent years, this does not necessarily mean that these processes are simply replicating earlier capitalist development in the developed countries; and, second, continued domination and subordination might exist in the international order, but the mechanisms through which these processes occur vary, and must be specified rather than read off from a general theory which has preconceived expectations about what these may be. And here, dependency might retain some utility, not as a static theory of underdevelopment, but through a recognition that that developing countries—the BRICs included—remain in a subordinate position in the international economy, and in some senses they remain strongly influenced by the core economies. Dos Santos (1970: 231) suggests that "(d)ependence is a conditioning situation in which the economies of one group of countries are conditioned by the development and expansion of others." This notion of dependence could of course be applied to any country, as all countries are in some sense dependent on others (Bernstein 1979). As we will see, the USA is dependent on Chinese capital. But as we will also see in the chapters that follow, some forms of dependency are more significant than others. The next section makes some preliminary observations concerning the rise of the BRICs and how this might relate to the discussion so far.

## Modernisation, Dependency and the BRICS: Some Preliminary Observations

So far this chapter has considered some data on the rise of the South, different IR theories and how they respond to this rise, and particularly China's leadership of a rising South, and debates over the question of development. We have seen that the liberal and realist debate is in many respects one about how the USA should respond to this rise, and thus how, in terms of our framing device outlined in the last section, this conforms to a modernisation or convergence-based approach to development. The rest of the book takes issue with these assumption, through detailed empirical analysis and theoretical reflection. This final section starts this task, and provides a broad overview of the rise of the BRICs with particular reference to the involvement of these countries in the rest of the South, and also with most attention period to the period up to 2008 (the post-2008 period is analysed in depth in later chapters). The purpose of this brief discussion is to establish some preliminary observations which suggest that the discourse of rise of the South should be treated with some caution.

In the case of China, if we consider, for example, its FDI stock in Africa, this reached \$7.8 billion by the end of 2008 (around 4% of

China's total), compared to (in 2003) $30 billion from the UK, $19 billion from the USA, $11.5 billion from France (Ayers 2013: 230). Since the 2008 crisis Chinese investment has increased in significance, especially compared to the USA but we should still not exaggerate its significance, in terms of both "quantity" and "quality." Thus, from 2000 to 2010 around 75% of China's FDI to Africa was in oil (from 2000 to 2010), which might suggest that China's interests is, to cite Rotberg (above), "extractive." However, the comparable figure for OECD countries was actually 85% (Ayers 2013: 231). In terms of trade, China is a growing market for sub-Saharan African exports, but in 2008 it still only accounted for 10% of its total exports (Ayers 2013: 231), though again this changed significantly in the post-crisis era (see Chap. 4). Finally, in 2007, though the data is not completely reliable and the figures reflect in part different definitions of grants and concessional loans (see above), Chinese aid stood at $1.4 billion, which compared to $30.7 billion in OECD grants to Africa, together with a further $11.8 billion in public and private bilateral loan agreements (Chin 2012: 581–2; Ayers 2013: 231). Although, as later chapters show, there have been some changes since the 2008 financial crisis, the picture prior to this still suggests that we need to be careful not to exaggerate China's involvement in parts of the global South (see Chap. 4).

Moreover, the Chinese Communist Party's image of itself as the saviour or friend of the "third world" is not shared by everyone. Mallam Sanusi, Governor of the Central Bank of Nigeria, argued in March 2013 that "China takes from us primary goods and sells us manufactured ones. This was also the essence of colonialism … China is a major contributor to the deindustrialisation of Africa and thus African underdevelopment" (cited in Taylor 2014: 14). Commodity prices have certainly been high in the period preceding the financial crisis, and after a collapse in 2008–09, recovered, only to fall back again from 2012 (see Table 4.2). Whatever the fate of commodity prices (see Chap. 4), development based on dependence on the export of primary commodity prices is precarious, not only because prices may fall and the commodities in question might account for a large proportion of export earnings, but also because primary goods production tends to be characterised by low productivity and limited spin-offs within economies. This is in contrast to (some) manufacturing sectors, and for Africa as a whole, the share of manufacturing in GDP fell from 15% in 1990 to 10% in 2008 (Taylor 2014: 9). In terms of employment growth over this period, manufacturing has been 11th out of 12 sectors, with only public administration behind it (Taylor 2014: 9). Indeed, for all the talk of Africa rising (Radelet 2010; Rotberg 2013) in recent years, if we break down growth rates within the continent and exclude those exporting petroleum and those affected by conflict, then the annual average growth rates for the "miracle" period from 2004 to 2008 was little different from annual average growth rates for the previous ten years (Weeks 2010: 6).

In Latin America, China is principally interested in its primary products. From 1990 to 2008, the share of primary products in the region's exports to China increased from 40.2 % to 71.9 %, while its share of manufacturing in exports to the rest of the world increased in the same period (Jenkins 2012: 1334). Moreover, while Chinese demand has been useful in facilitating price increases, we should still be careful not to exaggerate the significance of China in the region.[4] In 2010, just over 8 % of the region's exports went to China compared to 41 % to the USA, and 13 % to the European Union (EU). Thus in 2009 while exports to the USA fell by 26 % and to the EU by 28 %, they increased to China by 7.5 %. But this increase translated into an increase of exports to China of $3.6 billion, and a fall to the rest of the world of $200 billion (Jenkins 2012: 1353–4). However, as we will see in Chap. 4, slower growth in the USA and EU since the financial crisis has increased the significance of China for the developing world, at least in the short term. Thus, in the immediate post-crisis years China accounts for $3 of new investment in Africa compared to the USA' one dollar. Nonetheless, before the crisis there was good reason for some caution in discussing—and not exaggerating—the role of China in Africa.

What then of the other BRIC countries? Brazil has also increased its engagement with the rest of the South. For example, broadly coinciding with Lula's presidency (2003–10), trade increased with Africa substantially, from around $4.2 billion in 2000 to 27.6 billion in 2011. Much of this was framed in terms of growing South–South cooperation, and Brazil's cultural linkages with Africa, and in particular the fact that over half of Brazilians are descendants of African slaves (Skidmore 2010: 5). In the post-war period, Brazil's trade ties with Africa were dominated by links with apartheid South Africa and right wing leaders in Brazil even failed to condemn Portugese colonialism in Africa before 1974, so Lula's turn to the South and to the African continent should not be dismissed out of hand. Moreover, Brazilian links to Africa have not met with the degree of condemnation that is sometimes aimed at China (see above).

On the other hand. Brazil's links with the continent are not as extensive as those of China, and neither are they as altruistic as may first appear. In essence, under both Cardoso (1995–2003) and Lula (2003–10), Brazil has attempted to promote a more multilateral approach to international order, at least as much in an attempt to increase its own influence as to promote South–South solidarity. Contrary to the claims of some that we are now seeing the emergence of a new South (see Alden et al. 2012), the emergence of the India–Brazil–South Africa Forum in 2003 should be seen in this light. Mirroring domestic policy, Lula attempted to combine a policy of close ties to Washington and the neoliberal Washington Consensus, while presenting Brazil as a friend of the South (Ban 2013). Most specifically—and controversially—Brazil has been interested in the development of the hydrocarbon sector, and from 2007 to 2011 Brazil's main energy company Petrobas planned a doubling of investment in Africa in the hydrocarbon sector. This is part of a strategy to find alternative fuels for cars, and specifically ethanol. But this is controversial, particularly in the African continent where food security is unstable, because of its potential impact on both land use and food prices (Brown 2012: 37). However, even this development has altered as Brazil has become self-sufficient in oil (Guan 2010), and so for the period from 2012 to 2015, almost all of Petrobas' investment remained in Brazil (Taylor 2014: 47). This brief snapshot then suggests that Brazilian expansion is in some respects similar to the internationalisation associated with earlier capitalist developers, except insofar as the extent of Brazil's internationalisation remains much more limited. What it is not, then, is an alternative to the dominant neoliberal international order (Campos 2015).

India has used the rhetoric of South–South cooperation to widen its influence and pursue a more multilateral agenda within the institutions of global governance, especially since its period of rapid growth from 1991 onwards, and its growing awareness of its potential as a powerful nation in the international order. In the case of Africa, India has highlighted its common colonial background, and talked the language of solidarity. Trade between India and the African continent has also grown, from a value of $3.39 billion a year in 2000 to over $70 billion by 2013 (Taylor 2014: 86). There has also been a significant growth of foreign investment from India, for instance, by Tata, which is a major investor in South Africa. In terms of trade, primary commodity exports are central for India, and in 2010 they constituted 91 % of Africa's exports to India (Taylor 2014: 91), a figure which may actually increase given India's import energy dependence, and the attraction of Africa as a source of oil, not least as only two African states (Anglola and Nigeria) are OPEC (Organisation of Petroleum Exporting Countries) members subject to OPEC quota agreements.

Russia is far less involved in the South than the other BRIC countries, although there are some small signs of change in this regard. The Soviet Union had quite close historical ties to a number of African countries, giving support to a number of anti-colonial nationalist leaders and consistently opposing the apartheid regime in South Africa, unlike a number of Western countries. However, in the Yeltsin era (1991–99) aid was cut, African states were asked to repay their debt, and trade between Russia and Africa contracted, from $1.3 billion in 1990 to $740 million by 1994 (Taylor 2014: 59). However, following economic recovery from around 2000, and Russia's emergence as a major energy producer, there has been some renewal of interest in the continent. In 2009, the main Russian energy producer, Gazprom, entered into a partnership with the Nigerian National Petroleum Company and with the Algerian firm Sonotrach, in both cases to explore and commercialise gas supplies (Taylor 2014: 66). This growing interest in African energy supplies should, however, be put into context and Russia's interest in the continent remains relatively minor to date. Thus, in 2011, Russia accounted for only 1 % of Africa's merchandise exports to the BRIC countries (Taylor 2014: 71).

This brief discussion suggests that there is little evidence that China or the other BRICs (or in this case, BRICS) are behaving in a more progressive way than the Western world in the global South. Some critics, including NGOs and social movements at a BRICS counter-summit in Durban in 2013, even went so far as to argue that the BRICS represent a sub-imperialism, in which these more powerful nations in the developing world in effect exploit and subordinate weaker nations in the global South (Bond and Garcia 2015). In some respects then, the BRICS are simply weaker imperialists, part of the neoliberal international order. This is not to say that they are simply the same (see Kiely 2015: Chap. 3). For instance, in terms of aid, there are significant differences and the conditions attached to many Western loans, which promote privatisation and liberalisation, do not exist in the case of Chinese aid. But it is also clear that Chinese aid does come with conditions, Chinese employment practices are no better than those of many Western multinational companies (or their local subcontractors), and—like the other BRIC countries—investment is largely reflective of China's interests rather than designed to foster some wider South–South solidarity. Perhaps above all, China is interested in promoting a pattern of trade with the rest of the South which echoes earlier periods of Western colonialism, whereby the former develops industries and relies on raw materials from the latter. Seen in this way, while neoliberalism might kick away the ladder and condemn later developers to lower-value production, so too does China. Indeed, China is quite clear that what it wants from the rest of the South is primary commodities to fuel its manufacturing boom. This does not preclude investment (and aid) in infrastructure, but China's manufacturing growth has impacted negatively on other parts of the South. In the first ten months of 2005, following the liberalisation of clothing and textiles that replaced the old protectionist regime under the Multi-Fibre Agreement, African exports in those sectors fell by as much as 11% (Kaplinsky and Morris 2008). And the share of manufacturing value added in GDP in Latin America and the Caribbean fell from 19% in 1990 and 19% in 2000 to 16% by 2013. In sub-Saharan Africa the corresponding figures were 15% in 1990 and 13% in 2000 to 11% by 2013 (Rodrik 2015: Table 1). Rodrik (2015) has called this phenomenon "premature industrialisation." This brief discussion shows that there has been increased involvement by China and the other BRICs in the South. In terms of the debate over the desirability of the rise of a Chinese-led alternative to US hegemony, this brief survey has suggested that the positions of both those that welcome China's rise and those that see it as cause for regret are problematic. This is not the place for a full analysis of the US-led, post-Washington Consensus (see Kiely 2007), but there are strong arguments which suggest that this has had in many respects a problematic and indeed poor development record. In particular, and in keeping with the argument that is at least implied in this book, it can be argued that the neoliberal order has in effect acted to deprive developing countries of the right to promote protectionist industrial policies, and these are necessary in order to promote dynamic industries and indeed dynamic comparative advantage. Now of course this might beg the question of whether *all* countries can be winners within this discourse of competitiveness (see Davies 2014: Chap. 4), but for our purposes we just need to emphasise how this is even less likely when countries are left to specialise in producing low-value goods.

There is a further, related point here, which is that the argument that the rise of the South is part of a wider process of the diffusion of manufacturing is one-sided, and in some respects simply wrong. If we examine the rise of manufacturing in the South in recent years, it is highly uneven within countries, but also between countries, and only Asia shows evidence of a clear upward trajectory in this regard. Using constant (2005) US dollars as a yardstick, Rodrik (2015: Table 1) has calculated the regional share of global manufacturing value added from 1970 to 2013. The USA saw a decline from 26% to 19% in those years; Western Europe saw a decline from 24% to 13%; Latin America and the Caribbean saw no change, with a 6% share for both years; Asia (except China) saw an increase from 15% to 26%; China saw an increase from 0% to 18%; and sub-Saharan Africa saw no change with both years amounting to 1% of global manufacturing vale added. Perhaps even more significant were the changes in those years in the share of manufacturing value added in each country's GDP: the USA remained constant at 13%; Western Europe saw a decline from 22% to 18%; Latin America and the Caribbean saw a *decline* from 20% to 16%; Asia (except China) saw an increase from 16% to 20%; and sub-Saharan Africa saw a *decline* from 14% to 11%. These figures certainly show a falling global share of manufacturing value added for the USA, but for much of the South, the share remains small and far lower than that of the USA and Europe. Moreover, if we accept the argument that manufacturing is important because of its relative dynamism and capacity for linkages compared to primary good production, then the decline in the contribution of manufacturing value added in Latin America, the Caribbean and sub-Saharan Africa is problematic. Moreover, the share of manufacturing value added in GDP in the USA has not declined, which suggests that insofar as deindustrialisation has taken place in the USA, it is at least in part because of some productivity increases, at least when compared to deindustrialisation in part of the global South (and we might add that profitability in the USA and elsewhere in the global North has been revived because of stagnant real wages). The much trumpeted decline in manufacturing employment in the USA and elsewhere in the global North must partly be explained by higher productivity and a shift to services, though the global strategies of US multinational companies is also important as we will see in the next chapter. In contrast, for parts of the South, deindustrialisation is occurring at historically lower rates of per capita income than those of the now developed countries, and therefore the possibilities associated with higher productivity, employment, tradability in the world market, linkages and so on, are undermined.

Thus even in the era of a rising South, it appears that the diffusion of manufacturing remains limited. This can partly be explained by the competitive advantages enjoyed by earlier developers over later ones. The high rates of productivity, linkages and spin-offs generated by dynamic industrialisation processes are difficult to generate in relatively open markets because already established producers enjoy competitive advantage over late developers, which is reinforced by the shift towards more open markets, which undermined the capacity of later developers to build up industries through protectionist measures. Indeed, the falling share of manufacturing value added for both Latin America and the Caribbean, and sub-Saharan Africa, was most marked in the period after 1980, when both regions shifted to more neoliberal policies. For Latin America and the Caribbean, the share of manufacturing value added in GDP declined from 20% in 1980 to 16% in 2013, and the global share of manufacturing value added fell from 8% to 6% in the same period. For sub-Saharan Africa the corresponding figures were 15% and 11%, and a constant of 1% in 1980 and 2013 for global share of manufacturing value added (Rodrik 2015: Table 1).

Gallagher and Porzecanski (2010: 31–2) suggest that more than 80% of manufacturing exports from Latin America were threatened—directly and indirectly—by completion from Chinese manufacturing exports, either into the Latin American market or in other markets where China has increasingly undermined manufacturing competitors. The counter to this argument is that in some respects this has been a relationship of mutual advantage as developing countries (including Brazil and Russia) have benefited from high commodity prices, which in turn have been high in part because of demand from China. But, as was suggested above, this is a precarious strategy for countries that come to increasingly rely on exports from one or two primary commodities, especially if those export prices decline. And this is precisely what has happened in recent times and is a central part of the story of the shift from emerging markets boom to emerging markets crisis, as we will see in Chap. 4. Finally, and not unrelated to this point, there is the argument that the question of desirability, while important, should not lose sight of the question of actuality, and whether the South has risen as much as is often suggested. Thus in terms of our earlier discussions in this chapter, it may be the case that the rise of the South differs among countries within it, and that those leaders (the BRICs) behave in ways not unlike the leading states of the global North, particularly in terms of questions of political economy. But, also, it may be the case that even those leading states in the South remain in some respects dependent in the international order. This chapter has taken up this story, quite tentatively and briefly, but it is now time to consider this in more depth, especially in the next two chapters. Chapter 3 does this by looking at corporate power and globalisation, and specifically the continued centrality of US capital in the international order, while Chap. 4 looks at the fortunes of the global South both before and after the global financial crisis of 2008.

## Conclusion

This chapter has examined various theoretical positions on both IR and development, and briefly applied them to the question of the rise of the BRIC. As should be clear, what much of this debate is about is whether the rise of the BRICs is a welcome phenomenon or not. But we have also suggested that much of this is about the question of welcome for whom? Thus, we have liberal internationalists who largely welcome their rise, while realists are (usually) more sceptical but much of this is about realism and liberal internationalism *from the standpoint of the USA*. On the other hand, more critical approaches linked to versions of WST and dependency welcome the rise of the BRICs as it challenges the Western-dominated international order. At the same time, much of this debate is related to questions of development, and in the final section I introduced the idea that, for all the problems with both approaches, modernisation and dependency may be useful *framing devices* for examining the rise of the BRICs. On the face of it, the rise of the BRICs is about acceptance of modernisation and then responding to the question of whether or not this is desirable for the West (I leave aside the question of what we mean by the West and, indeed, which people in the West). But at the end, I suggested something which appears to be quite counterintuitive, which is that there may be a case for thinking about the rise of the South, the BRICs and even in some respects China, partly through the lens of the idea of dependency. This is taken up in the chapters that follow.

## Notes

1. The reasons why this is so vary for realists (see Waltz 1979; Morgenthau 2005).
2. There are of course more nuanced positions, which recognise the limits of the rise of the South but usually accept to some extent arguments around US decline (see, for instance, Rucki 2011; and on the question of hegemony, compare with Saull 2012). It should be clear in the argument that follows that too much of the declinist literature fails to take account of the specific nature of US hegemony and how it is closely connected to economic globalisation.
3. None of this is intended to paint a picture of Western investment as somehow better than Chinese investment. In the case of copper, Chinese investment is much lower than Western investment and this might be one reason why wages are lower in Chinese mines. Moreover, there are serious

issues around tax avoidance and transfer pricing by Western companies. The point in the text is made merely to question the view that Chinese aid and investment is somehow better than that originating from the West, but equally this does not mean that Western investment and aid is better.

4. This point applies also to the fact that while commodity price increases helped to promote growth, they alone are not the only cause that needs to be considered. See Rosnick and Weisbrot (2014).

## References


Alden, C., S. Morphet, and M. Vieira. 2012. *The South in World Politics*. Basingstoke: Palgrave.

Amsden, A. 1989. *Asia's Next Giant*. Oxford: Oxford University Press.

Arrighi, G. 2007. *Adam Smith in Beijing*. London: Verso.

Ayers, A. 2013. Beyond Myths, Lies and Stereotypes: The Political Economy of a "New Scramble for Africa". *New Political Economy* 18(2): 227–257.

Ban, C. (2013) 'Brazil's liberal neo-developmentalism', *Review of International Political Economy* 20(2): 241–55.

Bernstein, H. 1979. Sociology of Development versus Sociology of Underdevelopment. In *Development Theory: Four Critical Essays*, ed. D. Lehmann, 77–106. London: Frank Cass.

Bin Wong, R. 1997. *China Transformed*. Ithaca: Cornell University Press.

Bond, P., and A. Garcia (eds.). 2015. *BRICS: An Anti-Capitalist Critique*. London: Pluto.

Booth, D. 1985. Marxism and Development Sociology: Interpreting the Impasse. *World Development* 13(8): 761–787.

Bremmer, I. 2010. *The End of the Free Market*. New York: Portfolio.

Breslin, S. 2011. The "China Model" and the Global Crisis: From Friedrich List to a Chinese Mode of Governance? *International Affairs* 87(6): 1323–1343.

Brown, L. 2012. *Full Planet, Empty Plates*. New York: Norton.

BRICS (2013) 'Fifth BRICS Summit', available at http://www.brics5.co.za (Accessed June 6, 2015).

Campos, P.H. 2015. The Transnationalization of Brazilian Construction Companies. In *BRICS: An Anti-Capitalist Critique*, eds. P. Bond and A. Garcia, 148–161. London: Pluto.

Chandler, D. 2005. *From Kosovo to Kabul*. 2nd ed. London: Pluto.

Chang, H.-J. 2002. *Kicking Away the Ladder*. London: Anthem.

Chang, H.-J. 2007. *Bad Samaritans*. London: Random House.

Chase-Dunn, C. 2013. BRICS and the Potentially Progressive Semi-Periphery. *Pambazuka News*, March 19. http://www.pambazuka.org/en/category/features/86647/print. Accessed 5 Mar 2015.

Chin, G. 2012. China as a "Net Donor": Trading Dollars and Sense. *Cambridge Review of International Affairs* 25(4): 579–603.
Chomsky, N. 2002. *The Umbrella of US Power*. New York: Seven Stories Press.
Cooper, R. 2003. *The Breaking of Nations*. New York: Atlantic.
Council on Foreign Relations. 2006. More than Humanitarianism: A Strategic US Approach to Africa. Independent Task Force Report No. 56. www.cfr.org/africa/more-thanhumanitarianism/p9302. Accessed 13 Apr 2014.
Cox, R. 1981. Social Forces, States and World Orders: Beyond International Relations Theory. *Millennium* 10(2): 126–155.
Davies, W. 2014. *The Limits of Neoliberalism*. London: Sage.
Desai, R. 2012. The West Must Wake Up to the Growing Power of the BRICS. *The Guardian*, April 1.
Desai, R. 2013. The BRICS Are Building a Challenge to Western Economic Supremacy. *The Guardian*, April 2.
Deudney, D., and G.J. Ikenberry. 1999. The Nature and Sources of a Liberal International Order. *Review of International Studies* 25(2): 179–196.
Dirlik, A. 2006. Beijing Consensus, Beijing 'Gongshi.': Who Recognizes Whom and to What End? http://www.ids-uva.nl/wordpress/wp-content/uploads/2011/07/9_Dirlik1.pdf. Accessed 6 Feb 2013.
Dollar, D., and A. Kraay. 2002. Growth Is Good for the Poor. *Journal of Economic Growth* 7: 195–225.
Dos Santos, T. 1970. The Structure of Dependence. *American Economic Review* 60(May): 231–236.
Escobar, P. 2013. Brazil, Russia, India, China and South Africa: BRICS Go over the Wall. *Asia Times*, March 27, 2013. http://www.atimes.com/atimes/World/WOR-01-260313.html. Accessed 26 Mar 2015.
Evans, P. 1995. *Embedded Autonomy*. Princeton: Princeton University Press.
Financial Times. 2011. The End of Hegemony. September 6.
Fine, B., and J. Saraswati (eds.). 2013. *Beyond the Developmental State*. London: Pluto.
Foot, R. 2006. Chinese Strategies in a US-Hegemonic Global Order: Accommodating and Hedging. *International Affairs* 82(1): 77–94.
Frank, A.G. 1969. *Capitalism and Underdevelopment in Latin America*. New York: Monthly Review Press.
Frank, A.G. 1998. *Re-Orient*. Berkeley: University of California Press.
Gallagher, K., and R. Porzecanski. 2010. *The Dragon in the Room*. Stanford: Stanford University Press.
Giddens, A. 2000. *The Third Way and Its Critics*. Cambridge: Polity.
Goldman Sachs. 2010. Is This the "BRICs Decade". *BRICs Monthly* 10(3): 1–4.
Guan, E. 2010. Understanding Brazil's Oil Industry: Policy Dynamics and Self-Sufficiency. *Journal of Emerging Knowledge on Emerging Markets* 2: 26–40.
Halper, S. 2010. *The Beijing Consensus*. New York: Basic.

Hameiri, S., and L. Jones. 2016. Rising Powers and State Transformation. *European Journal of International Relations* 18(1): 53–75.
Hung, H.F. 2016. *The China Boom: Why China Will Not Rule the World*. Cambridge: Harvard University Press.
Huntington, S. 1968. *Political Order in Changing Societies*. New Haven: Yale University Press.
Ikenberry, G.J. 2008. The Rise of China and the Future of the West: Can the Liberal System Survive? *Foreign Affairs* 87(1): 23–37.
Jenkins, R. 2012. Latin America and China—A New Dependency? *Third World Quarterly* 33(9): 1337–1358.
Kagan, R. 2012. *The World America Made*. New York: Knopf.
Kaplinsky, R. and M. Morris (2008) 'do the Asian drivers undermine export oriented development in Latin America?', *World Development* 36(2): 254–73.
Kennedy, S. 2010. The Myth of the Beijing Consensus. *Journal of Contemporary China* 19(65): 461–477.
Keohane, R.O., and J.S. Nye. 1977. *Power and Interdependence: World Politics in Transition*. 4th ed. Boston: Longman.
Khanna, P. 2009. *The Second World*. Harmondsworth: Penguin.
Kiely, R. 2007. *The New Political Economy of Development*. Basingstoke: Palgrave.
Kiely, R. 2010. *Rethinking Imperialism*. Basingstoke: Palgrave.
Kiely, R. 2015. *The BRICs, US 'Decline' and Global Transformations*. London: Palgrave.
Kirshner, J. 2010. The Tragedy of Offensive Realism: Classical Realism and the Rise of China. *European Journal of International Relations* 18(1): 53–75.
Kitching, G. 1982. *Development and Underdevelopment in Historical Perspective*. London: Methuen.
Knight, J. 2014. China as a Developmental State. *The World Economy* 37(10): 1335–1347.
Kohli, A. 2004. *State Directed Development*. Cambridge: Cambridge University Press.
Lal, D. 1984. *The Poverty of 'Development Economics'*. London: Institute of Economic Affairs.
Lee, C.K. 2014. The Chimera of Global Convergence. *New Left Review* 87(2): 81–96.
Lundestad, G. 1998. *'Empire' by Integration: The United States and European Integration, 1945-1997*. Oxford: Oxford University Press.
Mahbubani, K. 2008. *The New Asian Hemisphere*. New York: Public Affairs.
Mearsheimer, J. 2001. *The Tragedy of Great Power Politics*. New York: W.W. Norton.
Mearsheimer, J. 2006. China's Unpeaceful Rise. *Current History* 105(April): 160–162.
Moravcsik, A. 1997. Taking Preferences Seriously: A Liberal Theory of International Politics. *International Organization* 51(4): 513–553.

Moravcsik, A. 2008. The New Liberalism. In *The Oxford Handbook of International Relations*, eds. C. Reus-Smit and D. Snidal, 234–254. Oxford: Oxford University Press.

Morgenthau, H. 2005. *Politics among Nations*. 7th ed. New York: McGraw Hill.

Mulvad, A. 2015. Competing Hegemonic Projects within China's Variegated Capitalism: 'Liberal' Guangdong vs. 'Statist' Chongqing. *New Political Economy* 20(2): 199–227.

Navarro, P. 2007. *The Coming China Wars: Where They Will Be Fought, How They Can Be Won*. Upper Saddle River, NJ: Financial Times Press.

Nolan, P. 2012. *Is China Buying the World?* Cambridge: Polity.

OECD. 2010a. *Perspectives on Global Development, 2010, Shifting Wealth*. Paris: OECD Development Centre.

OECD. 2010b. Perspectives of Global Development, 2010, Shifting Wealth: Summary. http://www.oecd.org/dev/pgd/45451514.pdf. Accessed 26 Jan 2013.

O' Neill, J. 2001. Building Better Global Economic BRICs. Goldman Sachs Global Economics Paper no. 66, pp. 1–16.

O' Neill, J. 2013. *The Growth Map*. London: Portfolio Penguin.

O'Neill, J. 2014. The MINT Countries: The Next Economic Giants. http://www.bbc.co.uk/news/magazine-25548060. Accessed 28 Feb 2014.

O'Neill, J., D. Wilson, R. Purushothaman, and A. Stupnytska. 2005. How Solid Are the BRICs? Goldman Sachs Global Economics Paper no. 134, pp.1–24.

Pomeranz, K. 2001. *The Great Divergence: China, Europe and the Making of the Modern World Economy*. Princeton: Princeton University Press.

Prebisch, R. 1959. Commercial Policy in the Underdeveloped Countries. *American Economic Review* 44: 251–273.

Radelet, S. 2010. *Emerging Africa*. Washington: Center for Global Development.

Ramo, J. 2004. *The Beijing Consenus: Notes on the New Physics of Chinese Power*. London: Foreign Policy Centre.

Rachman, G. (2010) Zero Sum World (New York: Atlantic).

Rodrik, D. 2015. *Premature Deindustrialization*. Cambridge: Harvard University, unpublished paper.

Rosnick, D., and M. Weisbrot. 2014. Latin American Growth in the Twenty First Century. http://www.cepr.net/documents/terms-of-trade-2014-05.pdf. Accessed 5 Mar 2015.

Rostow, W. 1960. *The Stages of Economic Growth*. Cambridge: Cambridge University Press.

Rotberg, R. (ed.). 2008. *China into Africa: Trade, Aid and Influence*. Washington: Brookings Institution.

Rotberg, R. 2013. *Africa Emerges*. Cambridge: Polity.

Rucki, S. 2011. Global Economic Crisis and China's Challenge to Global Hegemony: A Neo-Gramscian Approach. *New Political Science* 33(3): 335–355.

Saull, R. 2012. Rethinking Hegemony: Uneven Development, Historical Blocs and the World Economic Crisis. *International Studies Quarterly* 56(2): 323–338.
Singer, H. 1950. The Distribution of Gains from Trade between Investing and Borrowing Countries. *American Economic Review* 40: 473–485.
Skidmore, T. (2010) *Brazil* (Oxford: Oxford University Press).
Subin, V. 2014. BRICS Viewed from Russia. *Pambazuka News*, March 20. http://www.pambazuka.org/en/category/features/86658/print. Accessed 26 Mar 2015.
Taylor, I. 2014. *Africa Rising?* London: James Currey.
The Economist. 2012. The Rise of State Capitalism. January 21.
UNCTAD. 2013. *World Investment Report 2013.* Geneva: UNCTAD.
UNCTAD. 2014a. *Trade and Development Report 2014.* Geneva: UNCTAD.
UNCTAD. 2014b. *World Investment Report 2014.* Geneva: UNCTAD.
UNCTAD. 2015a. *Trade and Development Report 2015.* Geneva: UNCTAD.
UNCTAD. 2015b. *World Investment Report 2015.* Geneva: UNCTAD.
UNCTAD. 2015c. UNCTAD Handbook of Statistics. http://unctad.org/en/pages/PublicationWebflyer.aspx?publicationid=1414. Accessed 19 Feb 2016.
UNDP. 2013. *Human Development Report 2013.* New York: UNDP.
US Census Bureau. 2015. Trade in Goods and Services with China. www.census.gov/foreign-trade/balance/c5700.html. Accessed 16 Feb 2015.
US Treasury Department. 2013. Major Foreign Holders of Treasury Securities. http://www.treasury.gov/ticdata/Publish/mfh.txt. Accessed 7 Mar 2014.
Wade, R. 1990. *Governing the Market.* Princeton: Princeton University Press.
Wallerstein, I. 1974. *The Modern World System*, vol. 1. New York: Academic Press.
Wallerstein, I. 2003. *The Decline of American Power.* New York: New Press.
Waltz, K. 1979. *Theory of International Politics.* New York: Random House.
Weeks, J. 2010. Growth and Employment in Africa. London: SOAS, CDPR, 1–51. http://jweeks.org/2010%20Growth%20and%20Employment%20in%20Africa.pdf. Accessed 22 Nov 2014.
World Bank. 2002. *Globalization, Growth and Poverty.* Oxford: Oxford University Press.
Yeyati, E., and T. Williams. 2012. Emerging Economies in the 2000s: Real Decoupling and Financial Recoupling. World Bank Policy Research Working Paper no. 5961, Washington.
Zhao, S. (2010) 'The China Model: Can it Replace the Western Model of Modernization', Journal of Contemporary China 19(65): 419–36.
Zhu, L. 2010. China's Foreign Policy Debates, Chaillot Paper No. 121, Paris, Institute for Security Studies, European Union, September [Online]. www.iss.europa.eu/uploads/media/cp121-China_s_Foreign_Policy_Debates.pdf. Accessed 8 Feb 2016.

CHAPTER 3

# Questioning the Rise of the South I: Economic Globalisation and US Power

**Abstract** This chapter is the first substantive chapter to address the rising South thesis. It does so by first examining the question of the political economy of globalisation and why—for all its difficulties—it is a useful concept for understanding changes in the international order in recent years. It then shows, however, that this does not lead to a "flat earth" globalisation (as neoliberals but also some transnational capitalism theorists suggest) because of the differential power of states, but also the differential power of capitals, which still retain some significant degree of nationality, even as they have "globalised." This is demonstrated through looking in depth at corporate ownership structures, and it shows how US capital continues to play a leading role in global capitalism, and that the significance of the BRICs, though growing, is still relatively small. This discussion is then used to revisit the questions of modernisation and dependency.

**Keywords** Globalisation • Corporations • Ownership • Dependency

This is the first substantive chapter which questions the rising South thesis in some empirical depth. It does so first through some consideration of the question of globalisation, with particular attention to political economy. In this section I show how this overlaps with liberal internationalist perspectives of interdependence, and how this, on the face of it, suggests a



R. Kiely, *The Rise and Fall of Emerging Powers*,
DOI 10.1007/978-3-319-34012-8_3

"flatter earth" in which capital has increasingly diffused throughout the globe. This is also a view associated with more radical views of transnational capitalism, which are also briefly considered. In some respects, this view is not necessarily wrong, and the work of Panitch and Gindin (2012) is briefly discussed to support a more nuanced version of this view. But it is then argued at the end of the first section that this is only part of the story, and following Panitch and Gindin (whose focus is mainly on the US state), I provide some preliminary evidence on foreign investment returns, which suggest a story not only of diffusion throughout the globe, but of inequality and unevenness alongside this diffusion. In particular, it is not only the US state but US capital which remains a leading force in the global economy, and this is demonstrated in the second section which provides a detailed empirical analysis to make this case, and in doing so make some comparisons with the BRICs. Finally, and briefly, I conclude by returning to the question of modernisation and dependency and specifically revisit the question of cores and peripheries in the global economy.

## The Question of (the Political Economy of) Globalisation

Globalisation has been defined as "the intensification of worldwide social relations and interactions such that distant events acquire very localized impacts and vice versa" (Held and McGrew 2007: 2). This relates to a "stretching of social, political and economic activities" and an "intensification and growing magnitude of interconnectedness" (Held and McGrew 2007: 2–3). These rather abstract definitions suggest a world in which interdependence has intensified in recent years—thus, for example, the 2008 financial crisis did not just affect the US housing market but had far greater implications. Indeed, as the next chapter will show, the degree of interdependence might be greater than that suggested by the rising South thesis, for one of the contentions made by this thesis is that the South has in some respects delinked from dependence on the North. This argument is questioned in the next chapter, but we are getting ahead of ourselves. For now, we might note that this emphasis on interdependence is not dissimilar to the liberal internationalist position outlined in Chap. 2.

What evidence then is there to support the argument that the world is increasingly interdependent? Held and his co-authors (1999) list a number of issues, such as increased capital flows, trade, migration, international institutions and global social movements. For our purposes, though, we need only consider the question of capital flows and trade.

Writing from a more radical position than Held et al., Bill Robinson's broadly Marxist work on transnational capitalism provides some useful evidence which demonstrates the reality of globalisation. For example, he shows that there has been an increase in direct foreign investment, including mergers and acquisitions between firms originating in different countries, the increased practice of subcontracting and outsourcing by companies to (local and foreign) suppliers, and the increase in trade between two or more subsidiaries of the same parent company. Thus, from 1996 to 2000, outsourcing by US firms increased from $100 billion to $345 billion, and was particularly common in call centres, graphic design, computer programming and accountancy (Robinson 2004: 18). Foreign direct investment (FDI) grew from $59 billion in 1982 to $1.45 trillion by 2013 (UNCTAD 2014: 2), a rate of growth much faster than that of world production or investment (Robinson 2004: 23–4; Dicken 2015: 19–21). Cross-border mergers and acquisitions grew from just 14 deals in 1980, to 9655 in 1999, and transnational companies grew in number from 7000 in 1970 to 60, 000 by 2000 (Robinson 2004: 58, 55), and perhaps as much as 82,000 parent companies controlling 810,000 foreign affiliates by 2009 (Dicken 2015: 20). One of the most significant developments is the rise of global production networks or commodity chains, whereby companies increasingly outsource different fragments of the production process across national borders. This is a development often missed by so-called globalisation sceptics, who argue that trade/GDP ratios in the current era of globalisation are not significantly higher than they were in the late nineteenth century or early twentieth century (Hirst et al. 2009: 34–5; Doogan 2009: Chap. 3). The actual data presented does actually show significant upward trajectories in trade/GDP ratios, not only from 1950, but also for most countries from 1913 (see Hirst et al. 2009: Table 2.5; also Dicken 2015: 18). Moreover, what is more significant is the ratio of FDI to GDP, and of merchandise trade to merchandise value added, which for most developed countries, has significantly increased since 1913 (see Feenstra 1998).

How then do we make sense of this order? Liberal internationalists and neoliberals (including third way variants) suggest that this reflects an increasingly flatter earth (Giddens 2000; World Bank 2002; Friedman 2005) in which all countries can take advantage of the opportunities presented by the global market. While the richer countries may have an advantage in higher technology products based on innovation, poorer countries have the advantage of lower costs, including labour and land costs. So long as countries open themselves up to globalisation, they can enjoy the benefits of economic growth and poverty reduction. This kind of argument is then applied to the BRICs to suggest that, in economic terms at least, their rise is a welcome development that presents opportunities for all countries in the international order (OECD 2010a, b; O' Neill 2013).

But it is not only liberal internationalist and neoliberal approaches which suggest a flatter earth. Some Marxist approaches argue that the world is not flatter in respect of growing inequalities within countries, but it is in the sense that the global diffusion of capitalism has eroded the geographical North–South divide. Thus in Hoogvelt's (2001: 64–5) words, "the geographic core–periphery polarization is being replaced by a social core–periphery divide that cuts across territorial boundaries and geographic regions." Hardt and Negri (2004: xii) also argue that "contemporary global order can no longer be understood adequately in terms of imperialism as it was practised by the modern powers, based primarily on the sovereignty of the nation-state extended over foreign territory." Paralleling this argument, Robinson's (2004: 4) theory of transnational capitalism argues that globalisation represents "an *epochal* shift" which is characterised as referring to "fundamental worldwide changes in social structure that modify and even transform the very functioning of the system in which we live." In this era of transnational capitalism, "local elites have sought, not a regional circuit of accumulation in rivalry with circuits elsewhere, but a complete *integration* into globalized circuits ... Capitalists with investments in the territory of the United States, for instance, carry passports from Germany, France, Saudi Arabia, Mexico, Japan, Brazil, Korea, and numerous other countries, and the US national state protects and promotes their investments" (Robinson 2004: 131). Specifically on the BRICs, Robinson (2015b: 4) argues that "(t)here are now TCC contingents in almost every country of the world—certainly they are present and entrenched in the states of the BRICS countries—whose interests lie in strengthening their national and regional staging platforms for ongoing global integration."

There is one further work which demands some consideration, not least because it accords with the argument made in the next section. This is the contention that in fact the USA remains the central hegemonic force in the international order. For Panitch and Gindin (2004: 49), the post-1945 international order "was defined above all by the American states successfully overcoming the earlier fragmentation of capitalism into rival empires. The unique informal empire it now fashioned was characterized, most notably, by the US state's economic penetration of, and close institutional linkages with, the other advanced capitalist states." For this approach, the Bretton Woods order of fixed exchange rates, neo-Keynesian expansionary policies, welfare states and (in the Third World) developmentalist states, was an era of transition (Panitch and Gindin 2012). In the post-war period the USA ran balance of payments deficits to stimulate the international economy with dollars. This period saw the expansion of trade and production, and a growing internationalisation of capital as multinational companies invested in a variety of countries. The very success of this so-called golden age (Glyn et al. 1992) stimulated not only the internationalisation of production, but the internationalisation of finance, including offshore banking and the Eurodollar market. This in turn stimulated financial accumulation, which increasingly bypassed the regulations that were essential to the financial repression of the neo-Keynesian era. At the same time, the US-led system facilitated the recovery and rise of competitors, which undermined US hegemony. The USA initially responded by continuing to run balance of payments deficits, which undermined the dollar link to gold and led to global inflation in the 1970s. But in 1971, the USA abandoned the fixed exchange rate system, which led to the gradual elimination of national and international controls on the movement of capital. Financial expansion soared in this context, with, for instance, all manner of hedge funds developing in response to the uncertainties caused by trading in fluctuating currency values. But these very same funds became a source of instability as they were also used to speculate against the price of certain commodities and currencies. The 1970s also saw the further stimulation of the market in international dollars, as oil producers placed their increased wealth in various financial institutions which then lent this money to Latin America in particular. From 1979, the USA responded to the inflationary crisis by massively increasing interest rates, which led to recession and unemployment in the developed world, and unsustainable debt in the developing world (Kiely 2005: Chap. 3). This laid the basis for a new round of liberalisation, of trade, investment and finance and the increased internationalisation of states as they opened themselves up to the global market, and gradually eroded capital controls, fixed exchange rates and protectionist trade measures.

Where Panitch and Gindin (2012) argue that this has indeed led to the making of a global capitalism, this is in contrast to Robinson's position in that the latter argues that this gives way to both transnational capital and an increasingly transnational state (Robinson 2015a). In terms of the former, Robinson (2014: 150) argues that "there exists a mounting body of counterevidence showing that both transnationally interlocking directorates and the multinational composition of boards of directors of the leading transnational corporations (TNCs) and corporate peak associations are increasing rapidly, and that there is an historical trend towards the organic transnational integration of corporate governance and decision-making structures." The question of corporate ownership is considered in the next section. This is not really the place for a full analysis of the state, but we can briefly observe that Robinson (2014: 162–4) places much emphasis on the transnational forces that exist within state–society complexes. This tends towards either an instrumentalist view of states, in which they are captured by transnational capitalist classes acting as a class for itself, or a functionalist view in which states simply must serve the needs of transnational capital because of its structural power. Joseph (2008: 82) instead suggests that "(r)ather than focusing at the level of actors as Cox and Robinson tend to do—thus getting sucked into a discussion about the formation of a transnational ruling class—it is better to focus on changes in forms of regulation and accumulation and the relationship of these hegemonic projects, state strategies and governmentality." For our purposes, however, we need to look in more depth at the question of corporate ownership, and this is considered in depth in the next section.

## Differential Power and Globalisation: The Question of Corporate Ownership

The discussion in the last section focused on the growing political–economic interdependence associated with globalisation, which is said to have eroded the global North–South divide. For neoliberals and liberal internationalists, globalisation lays the basis for opportunities for all states and individual actors to participate in world markets, while for theorists of transnational capitalism, this gives rise to arguments that regardless of location a transnational capitalist class is exploiting a globalised proletariat (Burbach and Robinson 1999). Both these approaches then are compatible with the view that a more interdependent global capitalism is an important conditioning factor for explaining the rise of the BRICs and of the South more generally. We have also seen that, from the more state-centric lens of realism, one central argument concerning the decline of the USA, and the rise of China (as part of the wider rise of the South), is that the USA runs annual trade deficits with China and indeed China is a major creditor of US debt. If we move away from state-centrism, this again could be said to reflect Chinese–US interdependence, and perhaps even asymmetrical interdependence in which China actually has more power than the USA.

On the other hand, all these contentions face a paradox. Recall the common objection to dependency theory, namely, that all countries are dependent in the world economy, and so dependency cannot be used to explain the subordinate position of the global South in the international order. In this account the USA is dependent on, or even perhaps subordinate to, China. However, recall also that I briefly suggested in Chap. 2 that perhaps some forms of dependence matter more than others. And here the question of US debt is significant, for the fact that the USA is a net debtor does not lead to the consequences that one would expect. The expectation is that any one single debtor pays more interest on its debts than it receives on its own investments. If, however, we take the US economy in the aggregate, and draw on Gourinchas and Rey's (2005) detailed comparative study of rates of return on US foreign investment overseas and foreign investment into the USA, then we can note that in fact the opposite is the case. In particular, they suggest that from 1960 to 2001 US overseas assets earned an annualised rate of return of 5.6 %, compared to foreigners earning 3.6 % on US assets. Moreover, in what is often described as a period of US decline, in the period after 1973 the gap on rates of return increased from 6.8 % for US capital overseas and 3.5 % for foreign capital in the USA (Gourinchas and Rey 2005: 10–11). Now of course the period covered does not include the rising South period which is our main point of consideration, and aggregating for a national economy in this way is an exercise fraught with difficulties. But at the same time, this discrepancy is still significant and in need of some explanation and—given that we are largely interested in the period since 2001—updating. This is the task in this section.

As we have already seen, a major reason why China has come to be regarded as a hegemonic challenger to the USA is the rise of Chinese eco nomic power. In terms of the rise of corporations, there is some evidence to support this case. Thus, from 2002 to 2011 the value of assets managed by the state-owned Assets Supervision and Administration Commission in China rose from 7.1 to 28 trillion RMB, and their revenues rose from

3.4 to 20.2 trillion RMB (Nolan 2014: 749). The number of companies from the South in the FT 500 increased from 8 in 2000 to 79 in 2010, and 89 by 2014 (Nolan 2012: 79; Financial Times 2014). On the other hand, if we examine the recent FT500 (2014) data, based on market capitalisation of leading corporations, then we can put the "decline" of the USA and the "rise" of China and the rest of the South into some kind of perspective. In terms of the top 20 in this list, 13 are from the USA and only 1 from China (Petrochina, which was ninth, compared to fourth the previous year). All of the top 8 (Apple, Exxon Mobil, Microsoft, Google, Berkshire Hathaway, Johnson and Johnson, Wells Fargo, General Electric) and 9 of the top 10 were from the USA (Wal-Mart was 10th, one place behind Swiss company Roche). In terms of the top 100, there were 45 US companies and 8 Chinese companies (including those officially located in Hong Kong). All but one of these companies was in oil, petroleum, gas, or banking, the exception being Tencent (PC software and services) at number 42. As for the rest of the rising South, the picture is even starker, even if we somewhat generously include South Korea and Taiwan (and as a BRIC country, Russia). South Korea has one company (Samsung at 18), Brazil has two (Amber at 54 and Petrobas at 90), Taiwan has one (Semi-Conductor Man at 67), Russia one (Gazprom at 83) and Saudi Arabia one (Saudi Basic Industries at 78). So, 14 companies are from the (broadly defined) global South, while the other 86 are all from the global North. India's top company, Tata stood at number 125. In terms of the top 500, 30 are from China or Hong Kong, while 202 are from the USA (Financial Times 2014). The aforementioned 89 from the South in 2014, including China and Hong, also include a number of companies from the Middle East, the first-tier East Asian newly industrialising countries, Russia and Israel, and 26 of the 89 are in the 401–500 ranking (Financial Times 2014).

What then of the question of corporate profitability, which Gourinchas and Rey's data highlight? US direct foreign investment tends to be more concentrated in profitable sectors, or it tends to take place within value chains where the most lucrative activity is in the hands of US companies. Thus, the World Economic Forum's annual report on global competitiveness[1] attempts to measure competitiveness through institutions, policies and so on. Some of these measures show a bias towards market friendly approaches to development, for instance, on property rights, so the value of the measurements is limited. Nonetheless, there is still some utility to the report, and the 2014–15 one focuses more explicitly on innovation, which is central to the focus of this section. The 2014–15 report put the USA at number 3 (up from 5 the previous year), behind Switzerland and Singapore, compared to China at 28, Russia 53, South Africa 56, Brazil 57 and India at 71, though Hong Kong was as high as 7 (World Economic Forum 2014). Post the financial crisis, China's position has barely shifted, and it stood at 26th in 2010–11 (Beausang 2012: 153). Specifically on innovation, in 2014–15 the USA stood at number 5 while China was 32 (World Economic Forum 2014). In the leading sectors in terms of innovation, such as nanotechnology, the European Union, Japan and the USA remain the world's leaders. In 2005 they filed 84 % of triadic patents, compared to just 2.6 % for the BRICs (Beausang 2012: 163). By 2010, the USA and Japan generated 60 % of triadic patents,[2] compared to 1.79 % for China (Starrs 2014: 95). In terms of Research and Development spending as a proportion of GDP, in 2013, the US figure was 2.806 % compared to China's 2.019 % and an OECD (Organisation for Economic Cooperation and Development) average of 2.398 % (OECD 2014). The European Commission carried out surveys on research and development spending in 2007 and 2011, and found that while the US share declined from 38.4 % to 34.9 %, Japan's share increased from 18.4 % to 21.9 % (Starrs 2014: 94). In fact, the only significant BRIC in 2011 was China, with a share of just 2.7 % (Starrs 2014: 94–5).

Starrs' (2013, 2014) important work on the leading corporations in the world economy is also relevant here. Using the Forbes Global 2000 as a benchmark, which is based on the assets, market value, profit and sales of the top 2000 corporations (Starrs 2013: 820–2; 2014: 84), he examines the national distribution of profit across the 25 broad sectors used by Forbes. He also compares distribution shares both before and after the financial crisis, using 2006 and 2012 (Starrs 2013: 820) and 2007 and 2013—plus where relevant 2010 (Starrs 2014: 84)—as years by which a pre- and post-crisis comparison can be made. Comparing 2007 and 2013, US leadership increased in absolute terms in five sectors: business and personal services (from 46% in 2007 to 54 % in 2013), casinos, hotels and restaurants (from 52 % to 56 %), computer hardware and software (from 70 % to 72 %), financial services (from 47 % to 52 %) and media (from 60 % to 69 %) (Starrs 2014: 85–6). In a further five sectors (aerospace and defence; food, beverages and tobacco; heavy machinery; retail; utilities), US leadership increased relative to its nearest competitor. In another five sectors (conglomerates; healthcare equipment and services; heavy machinery; oil and gas; transportation), US leadership declined after

**Table 3.1** Share of BRIC domiciled companies in Forbes Global 2000 by sector (*source*: author's adaptation of data from Starrs (2014: 88–9)

| *Sector* | *BRIC percentage Share in 2007* | *BRIC percentage share in 2013* | *China percentage share in 2013* |
|---|---|---|---|
| Banking | 8 | 42 | 32 |
| Construction | 1 | 32 | 28 |
| Forestry, metals and mining | 22 | 44 | n.d. |
| Real estate | 0 | 20 | 19 |
| Utilities | 5.2 | 20 | n.d. |
| Oil and gas | 21 | 34 | n.d. |

the financial crisis but recovered after 2010. In both 2012 and 2013, the USA was the leading country in 18 out of 25 sectors, and had a 40 % share in 10 of the 25 (Starrs 2013: 823; 2014: 87).

It is true that in this period, US shares have declined in around 10 sectors, and BRIC countries have advanced their profit share in 22 of the 25 sectors (Starrs 2014: 87). In six sectors there has been a significant increase (see Table 3.1). However, in three of these sectors (banking, construction and real estate), the rise of the BRICs is dominated by China, and this reflects the role of the Chinese state in finance, which in turn, in the context of a massive fiscal stimulus after the financial crisis (see further below) led to a boom in construction and real estate. The rise of Brazil, Russia and India in the other three sectors reflects high commodity prices, which is also discussed in the next chapter. In other words, there may be specific short-term reasons for the significant rise in these sectors, and as will be argued in the next chapter, these might be coming to an end. More generally, there is a wider pattern in which China's significance is largely because of the dominance of its own companies in its own domestic market, and not because of the rise of Chinese global companies. Thus, in 2011 China emerged as the world's largest PC market, but the Chinese profit share in this sector was just 2 %, compared to 72 % for US companies (Starrs 2014: 90; Nolan 2014: 752–4). Even then, foreign dominance within the Chinese market in some sectors is striking, with foreign firms accounting for around 70 % of the domestic automobile market (2011) and 87 % of the soft drinks market (2011), Google Android alone accounting for 86.4 % of the share of the Chinese smartphone operating systems market (2012) and Boeing supplying more than half of China's commercial airline fleet (Starrs 2014: 90–91; Nolan 2014: 751). In 2011, US companies had about $100 billion in FDI in China and Germany $33 billion. In high technology sectors foreign firms accounted for around two-thirds of value added, which included 71 % in electronics and telecommunications equipment and 91 per cent in the computer and office equipment sector (Nolan 2014: 752; Steinfeld 2010).

This is then partly a story of the rise of Chinese companies within China, albeit with a highly significant foreign presence in some sectors. But as we have seen, China is a significant exporter of goods. How then do we explain China's rise as an exporter and at the same time, the relatively insignificant presence of Chinese companies in global markets? This reflects China's role as an assembler of goods within the context of the rise of global production networks, as discussed in the last section. Thus, China is the world's largest exporter of electronics but its share in that sector in the Forbes 2000 list was just 4 % in 2012 and 3 % in 2013 (Starrs 2013: 821; 2014: 85). As argued in the previous section, this is precisely where the concept of globalisation does have considerable utility, for what we have seen in recent years is the growing fragmentation of production, so that different stages of the production process take place within different localities. This is not simply a process of internationalisation, but one of globalisation because it involves different stages of the production process carried out by the same company, either directly by use of subsidiaries or indirectly by use of subcontractors (Dicken 2015). Thus, in contrast to realist theories, the US trade deficit with China needs to be considered in this context because "we cannot possibly understand US–China trade dynamics without observing that between 40% and 70% of world trade in the early twenty first century was intra-firm or associational, that some 40% of exports from China came from TNCs based in that country and that much of the remaining 60% was accounted for by associational firms involving Chinese and transnational investors" (Robinson 2015: 10).

China's rise must therefore partly be explained by its role in a globalised system of manufacturing production. The corporate strategy of Apple (whose computers state that they are designed in the US and assembled in China) is particularly interesting in this regard. In the case of the Apple iPod classic, a 30gb iPod cost $299 in the USA in 2005. The approximate cost that Apple paid for the product from Hon Hai Precision Industry, a Taiwan-owned, company which uses its Chinese subsidiary, Foxconn, was $144. Of this, about 3 % went to the Taiwanese assembler operating in China, 51 % to the Japanese hard drive producer (assembled in

China using imported inputs), 3 % to the US semi-conductor designer and 2 % to the South Korean (owned and located) memory chip producer (see Linden et al. 2007: 6; Steinfeld 2010: 86; see also Froud et al. 2012). The Apple iPhone, launched in 2007, sold for $500 while the cost of manufacturing stood at $178.96. Chinese labour costs were around $6.50 for each phone, which constitutes just 3.6 % of the manufacturing cost (Xing and Detert 2010: 8). In 2011, Hon Hai Precision Industry's total profit was $2.6 billion, while Apple's was $33 billion (Starrs 2013: 819). Over the previous six years, Apple's share price rose more than ten-fold, while Hon Hai's fell by almost 80 % (Smith 2012: 90).

At the same time, while China's stock of outward FDI (including Hong Kong) has increased from $28 billion in 2000, to $366 billion in 2011, this was 29 % of the Netherlands total,[3] 27 % of France's total, 25 % of Germany's total, 21 % of the UK total and just 10 % of the US total (UNCTAD 2012: Annex, Table 1.2). Moreover, China's FDI presence in the advanced economies is very small: in 2011 its stock of FDI in the USA was $9 billion compared to the US stock of $100 billion in China; its stock of outward FDI in Germany was $2.4 billion compared to Germany's stock of around $33 billion in China; and Japan's stock of FDI in China was $85 billion, around 60 times greater than that of China's in Japan (Nolan 2014: 756).

It is often argued, not without justification, that focusing on the domicile of a particular company is misleading, because ownership of shares is dispersed across a variety of countries, which is an intrinsic part of the globalisation of production (Robinson 2014, 2015). However, in contrast to the transnational capitalist class thesis, share ownership is not as dispersed as is sometimes assumed. In particular, US ownership of foreign firms is greater than foreign ownership of US firms. The US share in cross-border merger and acquisitions alone was often more than 20 % in each individual country for the period from 2000 to 2009, while the *combined* foreign share (i.e. *all* foreign countries) in the USA was 16 % (Starrs 2013: 824). In the Forbes 500 for 2012, US firms combined owned 46 % of all publicly listed shares, which compared to 33 % of US domiciled firms (a total of 167 firms) and 22 % of global GDP (Starrs 2013: 824). In comparison, Japan, the second largest national owner, had just 7.7 %, and China had 29 firms in the top 500, 5.8 % of the total, and Chinese firms owned just 5.9 % of the top 500 shares (Starrs 2013: 824–5). In terms of national ownership, based on national ownership of the top 20 firms by region, US citizens owned 86 % of US domiciled shares, while in the EU the UK owned 15 % of EU member country domiciled shares, Germany 12 %, and France 11 %. The number one national owner in the EU was actually the USA at 24 % (Starrs 2013: 825). None of the BRIC countries, China included, own any significant proportion. In China, there are strict controls on foreign ownership and foreign owners account for very small share amounts on the Shanghai stock exchange. On the other hand, on the Hong Kong stock exchange, national ownership of non-controlling "H shares" are listed, and the USA, with 31 %, is by far the largest owner (Starrs 2013: 825).

In terms of finance, if anything concentration is even greater, though it is complicated by the fact that Britain also plays a lead role in that sector. However, it does so largely through close relations with the USA. Thus, for 2013 out of the top 100 hedge funds, with a total of $1.3 trillion of funds managed by these firms (over half of all assets managed by global hedge funds), 75 were located in the USA, 5 in the UK, 2 in Bermuda and all of the top 10 were either from the USA (six firms) or from the UK (four firms; Institutional Investor's Alpha 2013). In terms of investment banks, in 2013, six of the top ten were US, with one each from Switzerland, the UK, Germany and Canada but in the Swiss and German cases most of their activities were either in London or in New York (Financial Times 2013). In 2014, 9 of the top 10 and 17 of the top 20 largest private equity funds were all from the USA (PEI 2014).

One response to these figures is that they ignore client confidentiality in investment firms, and it is likely that US firms manage the wealth of foreign clients, who might be considered to be part of a transnational capitalist class. The fact that management of this wealth is usually by US companies is itself telling, but in any case Starrs (2013: 825) partially overcomes this problem by presenting data on the world's wealthiest individuals, as a proxy for the world's most significant investors. He finds that 42 % of the world's millionaires are US citizens and also estimates that 41 % of all global household assets are concentrated in North America (Starrs 2013: 826). Given the limited nature of some of the information from which he draws, there is some degree of guesswork in his findings, but we do know that US firms own around 46 % of the world's corporations, US citizens own most US domiciled company shares, and the USA is by far the most significant foreign owner of shares, so the data on millionaires and assets are likely to be fairly accurate. This suggests the central role of not only the US state in the international order, but also US capital. Robinson is of course correct that the international capitalist order is not reducible to US capital, and the capitalist classes of other countries are significant players. But the evidence presented in this section suggests that US capital is still the most significant player. Even more significant for our purposes, the role of the BRICs is comparatively far less significant.

In terms of the BRICS, and China in particular, there is one company which has to some degree bucked these trends, namely, Huawei. Around 65 % of Huawei's revenue in 2014 came from outside of China, and in the same year, it became the first Chinese company to secure a position in the Interbrand Top 100 global brands list (Interbrand 2014a, b). Initially its main focus was on the developing world market, with Africa accounting for one-third of its international sales and Nigeria alone accounting for three times more than the total European sales in 2004, but sales have risen significantly in the developed world since then (Nolan 2014: 761). Some argue that other companies will follow. Thus in 2014, the Chinese e-commerce Alibaba completed the biggest initial public offering (IPO) in history, and established a market capitalisation of $200 billion. The Chinese companies Baidu and Tencent are dominant in the Chinese social media and Internet games markets, and Xiaomi, a company less than five years old, has already established itself as a major played in the smartphone market. But we need to be careful here for while it is true that Huawei has gone some way to establishing itself as a global brand, its success in the US market has been limited, not least because the US state has used protectionist policies to limit its impact, all in the name of national security, as in the earlier cases like an attempted Chinese takeover of oil company Unocal, as well as Huawei's attempted takeover of Marconi, both in 2005 (Nolan 2014: 757–8). As for the other companies, in 2015 Alibaba faced a lawsuit in the USA over failing to disclose full information over its IPO, and Xiaomi faced similar difficulties in India, and its sales have been suspended pending the resolution of a patent dispute with Ericsson (The Register 2015; Pilling 2015). This suggests again that Chinese firms are far more successful within rather than beyond China, and the number one Chinese brand, China Mobile, is barely known outside of its home country, and benefits from enormous state protection in China (Arthur 2016; Hung 2016: 63). Finally, it should be noted that in 2010, the stock of China's non-financial outward FDI totalled $298 billion, less than that of Singapore. Moreover, almost two-thirds of this total is accounted for by investment to Hong Kong. If we therefore exclude Hong Kong, China's total outward FDI totalled $118 billion, less than one-tenth of its holdings of (low interest) US Treasury bonds at the time (Hung 2016: 121).

Moreover, it is perfectly possible to concede that at some point in the future, increasing numbers of Chinese firms will become important global players, but at the same time we must differentiate this from the much stronger argument that China's rise is undermining the economic hegemony of the USA. However, there is a further argument that we need to consider, which focuses more specifically on the longer-term effects of the financial crisis. This is the subject of the next chapter. Before moving on to consider this, however, we first need to take stock and relate the discussion in this chapter to a reconsideration of the ideas of modernisation and dependency. This is done in the next section.

## Conclusion: Corporate Ownership, Globalisation and Modernisation and Dependency Revisited

This chapter has argued that we can identify something called the political economy of globalisation, and this is part of the rise of multinational companies, the use of global production networks, the rise of global finance and thus the general intensification of capital flows across the world. The question then is the extent to which this global diffusion of capitalism has led to an *evening up* of inequalities in the world economy. For neoliberal and liberal internationalists this is indeed what has taken place. But we have also seen that for some Marxists, such as those associated with transnational capitalism, this is also deemed to have occurred, even as class inequalities have increased. For all their differences then, the rise of manufacturing in the South and the rise of the BRICs can be interpreted as part of this evening up process, or tendency towards convergence. None of this conforms to the rigid five-stage model associated with modernisation theory, and discussed in Chap. 2. However, as was argued in that chapter, we might usefully attempt to interpret the rise of the South and the BRICs in particular through the use of modernisation as a framing device, rather than a rigid theory.

But this chapter has suggested that while there has indeed been a diffusion of capitalism throughout the globe, this has not eliminated hierarchy within this context of intensified interdependence. In particular the internationalisation of capital has led to diffusion, but at the same time it has not eliminated hierarchy, and there are good grounds for suggesting that US capital remains the world's leader. This is not to say that nothing has changed from earlier eras of national capitals competing with each other in economic and geopolitical terms, as some dogmatic Marxist approaches contend (for a critique, see Kiely 2010), but it is to argue that the USA is still the leader within an increasingly global capitalism. Thus, in terms of global commodity chains, it appears that the increased use of such networks of production is central to the process of diffusion, but at the same time much of the most lucrative or profitable activity remains concentrated in the developed world, and above all in the USA. This argument suggests that there are good grounds for questioning not only the supposed decline of the USA, but also the rise of the South, China included. In terms of the framing devices identified in Chap. 2, this argument suggests some affinity with the idea of dependency. Again, this is not dependency in the static sense that the periphery does not change, and clearly there has been significant change as reflected in the (selective) rise of manufacturing and wider diffusion of capitalism. But in terms of the (changing forms of) hierarchy in the international order, we have identified some significant elements of domination and subordination. But this of course does not itself explain the specifics of the rise of the South in the period from the 1990s, but especially the 2000s, and even after 2009, which might still confirm the modernisation thesis. The next chapter carries out this task, and shows how the specific "virtuous" factors that facilitated the emerging markets boom then gave rise to "vicious" factors, which has led to the emerging markets crisis.

## Notes

1. This is not the place for a full discussion on the discourse of competitiveness. My use of this concept here is simply to highlight the continued leading role of US companies in the world economy.
2. These are patents registered at national patent offices and thus can be used as a kind of rough proxy for significant patents in terms of innovation, as opposed to relatively basic ones.
3. It should, however, be noted that the Netherlands figure is in many respects misleading owing to the fact that it is a country that acts as a conduit for foreign investment flows, and is in effect a "pass through" area of jurisdiction for foreign investment flows.

## References

Arthur, C. 2016. Xiaomi: It's China's Apple Though You've Probably Never Heard of It. *The Guardian*, January 16. http://www.theguardian.com/technology/2015/jan/16/xiaomi-chinas-equivalent-to-apple. Accessed 16 Jan 2016.

Beausang, F. 2012. *Globalization and the BRICs*. Basingstoke: Palgrave.

Burbach, R., and B. Robinson. 1999. The Fin de Siecle Debate: Globalization as Epochal Shift. *Science and Society* 63(1): 10–39.

Dicken, P. 2015. *Global Shift*. 7th ed. London: Sage.

Doogan, K. 2009. *New Capitalism?* Cambridge: Polity.

Feenstra, R. 1998. Integration of Trade and Disintegration of Production in the Global Economy. *Journal of Economic Perspectives* 12(4): 31–50.

Financial Times. 2013. League Tables: Investment Banking Review. http://markets.ft.com/investmentBanking/tablesAndTrends.asp?ftauth=1426510006710. Accessed 16 Mar 2014.

Financial Times. 2014. The FT Global 500. http://www.ft.com/cms/s/0/988051be-fdee-11e3-bd0e-00144feab7de.html#axzz3RLgneD1a. Accessed 16 Feb 2015.

Friedman, T. 2005. *The World Is Flat*. New York: Allen Lane.

Froud, J., S. Johal, A. Leaver, and K. Williams. 2012. Apple Business Model. CRESC Working Paper no. 111, Manchester, pp. 1–29.

Giddens, A. 2000. *The Third Way and Its Critics*. Cambridge: Polity.

Glyn, A., A. Hughes, A. Lipietz, and A. Singh. 1992. The Rise and Fall of the Golden Age. In *The Golden Age of Capitalism*, eds. S. Marglin and J. Schor, 39–125. Oxford: Clarendon.

Gourinchas, P-O., and H. Rey. 2005. From World Banker to World Venture Capitalist: US External Adjustment and the Exorbitant Privilege. http://socrates.berkeley.edu/~pog/academic/exorbitant/exorb_privilege_0804.pdf. Accessed 1 June 2013.

Hardt, M., and T. Negri. 2004. *Multitude*. New York: Penguin.

Held, D., and T. McGrew. 2007. *Globalization/Anti-Globalization*. Cambridge: Polity.

Held, D., A. McGrew, D. Goldblatt, and J. Perraton. 1999. *Global Transformations*. Cambridge: Polity.

Hirst, P., S. Bromley and G. Thompson (2009) *Globalization in Question* (Cambridge: Polity).

Hoogvelt, A. 2001. *Globalization and the Postcolonial World*. Basingstoke: Palgrave.

Hung, H.F. 2016. *The China Boom: Why China Will Not Rule the World*. Cambridge: Harvard University Press.

Institutional Investor's Alpha. 2013. Hedge Fund Ranking. http://www.institutionalinvestorsalpha.com/Research/4869/Hedge-Fund-100-Ranking.html. Accessed 16 Mar 2014.

Interbrand. 2014a. Interbrands 15th Annual Global Brands Report. http://interbrand.com/en/newsroom/15/interbrands-th-annual-best-global-brands-report. Accessed 10 Feb 2015.

Interbrand. 2014b. Rankings 2014. http://www.bestglobalbrands.com/2014/ranking/. Accessed 10 Feb 2015.

Joseph, J. 2008. On the Limits of Neo-Gramscian International Relations: A Scientific Realist Account of Hegemony. In *Gramsci, Political Economy and International Relations Theory*, ed. A. Ayers, 67–88. London: Palgrave.

Kiely, R. 2005. *The Clash of Globalisations: Neo-Liberalism, the Third Way and 'Anti-Globalisation'*. Leiden: Brill.

Kiely, R. 2010. *Rethinking Imperialism*. Basingstoke: Palgrave.

Linden, G., K. Kraemer, and J. Dedrick. 2007. Who Captures Value in a Global Innovation System? The Case of Apple's Ipod. Personal Computing Industry Center, Irvine, pp. 1–10.

Nolan, P. 2012. *Is China Buying the World?* Cambridge: Polity.

Nolan, P. 2014. Globalisation and Industrial Policy: The Case of China. *The World Economy* 37(6): 747–763.

OECD. 2010a. *Perspectives on Global Development, 2010, Shifting Wealth*. Paris: OECD Development Centre.

OECD. 2010b. Perspectives of Global Development, 2010, Shifting Wealth: Summary. http://www.oecd.org/dev/pgd/45451514.pdf. Accessed 26 Jan 2013.

OECD. 2014. Gross Domestic Spending on R and D. http://data.oecd.org/rd/gross-domestic-spending-on-r-d.htm. Accessed 13 Feb 2015.

O' Neill, J. 2013. *The Growth Map*. London: Portfolio Penguin.

Panitch, L., and S. Gindin. 2004. Finance and American Empire. In *The Socialist Register 2005*, eds. L. Panitch and S. Gindin, 46–81. London: Merlin.

Panitch, L., and S. Gindin. 2012. *The Making of Global Capitalism*. London: Verso.

PEI. 2014. The 2014 PEI 300. https://www.privateequityinternational.com/PEI/PEI_300_-_Top_50/. Accessed 16 Mar 2015.

Pilling, D. 2015. Corporate China Not Yet Ready to Rule the World. *Financial Times*, February 4.

Robinson, B. 2004. *A Theory of Global Capitalism*. Baltimore: Johns Hopkins University Press.

Smith, J. 2012. The GDP Illusion. *Monthly Review* 64(3): 86–102.

Starrs, S. 2013. American Economic Power Hasn't Declined—It Globalized! Summoning the Data and Taking Globalization Seriously. *International Studies Quarterly* 57(4): 817–830.

Starrs, S. 2014. The Chimera of Global Convergence. *New Left Review* 87(2): 81–96.

Steinfeld, E. 2010. *Playing Our Game*. Cambridge: Cambridge University Press.

The Register. 2015. Ericsson Drags Xiaomi Back to Court in India. http://www.theregister.co.uk/2015/02/09/ericsson_drags_xiaomi_back_to_court_in_india/. Accessed 10 Feb 2015.

UNCTAD. 2012. *Trade and Development Report 2012*. Geneva: UNCTAD.

UNCTAD. 2014. *World Investment Report 2014*. Geneva: UNCTAD.

World Bank. 2002. *Globalization, Growth and Poverty*. Oxford: Oxford University Press.

World Economic Forum. 2014. Global Competitiveness Report, 2014-2015. http://www.weforum.org/reports/global-competitiveness-report-2014-2015. Accessed 26 Mar 2015.

Xing, Y., and N. Detert. 2010. How the iPhone Widens the Trade Deficit with the PRC. ADBI Working Paper Series, no.257.

CHAPTER 4

# Questioning the Rise of the South II: From Emerging Markets Boom to Emerging Markets Crisis

**Abstract** The chapter examines the extent to which the 2008 financial crisis and its aftermath has altered the balance of power in the international order. It specifically challenges the view that 2008 signals a moment of both irreversible decline for the USA and the rise of the South. It first shows how the boom before 2008 rested on a number of specifics (China–US interdependence, primary commodity booms in the rest of the South, capital flows to the South) and how, after the crisis, recovery in the South also rested on a number of factors (capital flows to the South, renewed high commodity prices, China's stimulus). Drawing on the most up to date empirical material, the chapter then shows how this recovery in the South has come to an end, with falling primary commodity prices, capital inflows now becoming outflows, serious economic difficulties in China and slowdowns in growth in much of the South.

**Keywords** Financial crisis • Emerging markets boom • China • Commodity supercycle • Emerging markets crisis

This chapter examines the shift from what we might call the emerging markets boom of the 2000s, to what we can now see as an emerging markets crisis. This chapter therefore goes to the heart of the arguments presented in this book, namely, the questioning of the rising South discourse, and also secondarily the questioning of the extent of US decline. This task



R. Kiely, *The Rise and Fall of Emerging Powers*,
DOI 10.1007/978-3-319-34012-8_4

is undertaken in two main sections, each of which has subsections. The first section examines in more detail the specific reasons for the emerging markets boom, especially after 2002, and again from 2010 onwards. Through the use of two subsections, it particularly highlights the following: the importance of China's role in manufacturing, and its stimulus programme after the 2008 financial crisis; the primary commodity supercycle of high prices fuelled in part by demand from China, and the associated rise of South–South trade and the argument that this has involved the South's "delinking" from dependence on the global North. The chapter then moves on to show how these factors have now given way to a shift from boom conditions to something approaching a crisis for much of the global South. The first subsection therefore examines recent developments in China and its wider impact; the second subsection examines commodity prices; and, in shifting from a focus on primary commodity prices, the third question examines the decoupling question through an examination of capital flows and relates this to the slowdown in growth and recession in parts of the South.

## The Emerging Markets Boom

So far in this book, we have established that the rise of the South is closely linked to the rise of the BRICs, and above all China. We have also seen that some areas of the South have boomed because of high commodity prices and what has sometimes been called the commodity supercycle. These issues are examined in more depth in this section, in the period both before and after the 2008 financial crisis. After outlining and analysing these processes, this section then moves on to consider an influential argument which was central to the rising South thesis, namely, that the South had somehow decoupled or delinked from dependence on the global North, which in turn was linked to the increase in South–South trade in this period. These then are the three issues examined in this section (for a fuller background treatment of these, see Kiely 2015: Chaps. 4 and 5).

### *China and the World*

As earlier chapters argued, manufacturing is an important part of the development process because it can have far spin-offs for the rest of the economy which do not apply to, say, primary goods. One of the legacies of the colonial era was an international division of labour in which the global

North produced most of the manufactured goods in the world economy. Thus in 1939, 71 % of manufacturing production was concentrated in just four core countries, and 90 % in 11 countries from the core of the world economy (Dicken 2011: 14–15). The rise of manufacturing in (parts) of the developing world is therefore a central component of the rising South thesis.

One explanation for the increase in manufacturing in the South is that it has occurred as developing countries have liberalised their investment policies, and thus made it easier, and more desirable, for multinational companies to invest there. Earlier chapters showed the extent of the foreign investment boom since the early 1990s, and this has coincided with an increased share of global production, trade and investment in the developing world (see Chap. 2). Thus, in the period from 1990 to 2008, the share of foreign direct investment (FDI) in GDP increased from 5.8 % to 8.7 % in China, 2.1 % to 9.8 % in South Korea, 0.5 % to 9.9 % in India and 8 % to 18.3 % in Brazil (Dicken 2011: 22). We have seen how this in part reflects the global strategies of multinational companies and their use of global production networks, whereby different stages of the production process are utilised in different locations. On the other hand, we have also seen that we need to take some care in talking about a wholesale rise of manufacturing across the South as a whole. While much of the data demonstrates an increase in foreign investment, both globally and within the South, this alone does not tell us whether or not such investment is in manufacturing. Furthermore, as Chap. 2 argued, some parts of the developing world have in some respects *deindustrialised* in recent years, and it is only the Asian region, and above all China, which has seen significant growth in manufacturing. What we therefore need to focus on at this point is the rise of China, where rates of growth and foreign investment are indeed led by manufacturing.

In the period from 1993 to 2008, exports grew in real terms by about 500 % (Steinfeld 2010: 71). China's share of global exports was just 1.9 % in 1990, compared to 8.5 % for Japan, 11.6 % for the USA and 12.1 % for Germany. By 2005, the comparable figures were 7.3 % for China, 9.4 % for Germany, 5.7 % for Japan and 8.7 % for the USA. By 2010, post the crisis, the figures were 10.6 % for China, 8.1 % for Germany, 5.2 % for Japan and 8.6 % for the USA (Farooki and Kaplinsky 2012: 40). By 2010 then, China had emerged as the world's biggest exporter (Steinfeld 2010: 71). In the same period, China's share of global FDI accounted for 1.6 % of global flows in 1990, but this increased to 8 % by 2008 (Farooki and Kaplinsky

2012: 41). In 1983, direct foreign investment amounted to $1.73 billion spread over 470 projects; by 2006, $193 billion of FDI found its way to 27,514 projects (Steinfeld 2010: 72).

One of the most significant factors in China's rapid growth has been its export dependence. From 1965 to 2004, the combined export/GDP ratio for Japan, Taiwan and South Korea varied from around 10% to 20%, while China's by contrast was consistently between 20% and 30% from the early 1990s, and from 2000 to 2004, it increased to over 30% a year (Hung 2009: 8). In the period from 2002 to 2008, exports grew on average by 25% a year, while domestic consumption lagged behind growth. About one-third of GDP growth in China was directly due to exports, and in addition there were also substantial linkages and spin-offs arising from the multiplier effect of exports on domestic consumption and investment (Akyuz 2012: 27). In 2005, 82.9% of exports went to the North (including Eastern Europe), and 79.8% in 2007. Post the crisis, this figure had fallen, but it was still as high as 76.4% in 2010 (Akyuz 2012: 27–8). One of the most significant factors in terms of Chinese export patterns is that it is highly dependent on the USA and European Union (EU) markets. Indeed, if these two units are removed from the equation, then China (in both 2005 and 2010) had a trade deficit with the rest of the world. Thus in 2010 China's trade balance stood at a surplus of $143.3 billion, while its surplus with the USA was $201.2 billion and with the EU was $154.9 billion. Thus, its deficits with the rest of the world was over $200 billion, with much of this made up of deficits of around $79 billion each with both South Korea and Japan (Hung 2016: 129). This reflects China's continued subordinate role in global production networks, and fully accords with the argument outlined in the previous chapter.

At the same time, the growth of domestic consumption grew less rapidly than export growth. Consumption as a share of GDP averaged somewhere between 50% and 60% from 1965 to 2004 in Taiwan, South Korea and Japan. In China, in the early boom years of the 2000s, the corresponding figure was less than 40% and for all of the period it was below 50% (Hung 2009: 8). Even more notable was the decline on the share of wage income in China's GDP from 53% in 1998 to 41.4% in 2005 (Hung 2011: 219). It should be clear then that China's boom was led by manufacturing and was characterised by a high degree of dependence on exports to the developed world. This export-led growth led to enormous trade surpluses, and therefore was also a major factor in continued and growing trade deficits on the part of the USA. As we have seen, such deficits are a major factor used by a number of realists and world systems theorists to explain US decline (see Chap. 2), but the figures on China's own deficits with the rest of the world cited above put this argument into perspective. In contrast, some liberal internationalists (Dooley et al. 2009) suggested that this situation reflected greater interdependence, as China exported to the USA (and undervalued its currency to enable further exports), and generated enormous surpluses. Increased manufacturing meant that China could continue to absorb vast supplies of labour migrating from the countryside. Meanwhile, the USA benefited from cheap imports (reinforced by an overvalued dollar) generating current account surpluses. The overvalued US dollar meant that imports were cheaper in the USA, thus facilitating continued growing demand, not least in the context of stagnant real wages. In terms of deficits and surpluses, both sides benefited as China can continue to export to the USA, while the US deficits are financed in part by foreign creditors, among whom China (along with Japan) is the most significant. On the other hand, critics suggest that such a scenario was not sustainable because of problems faced by both sides. Much of the argument here was linked to the US decline thesis for it tended to emphasise the problems and relative weakness of the USA in this situation of interdependence, and implied that China might want to gain more from the purchase of US debt. In effect this would mean higher interest rates for Chinese (and other) creditors, but this would further weaken the US economy already "hollowed out" by manufacturing decline.

Much of this debate is implicitly one over the extent to which China is locked into the existing international order. This is also, however, a question of the way in which hegemony is exercised in such an order. In particular, given the fact that the US dollar remains the main international means of payment, and is the national reserve currency of the USA, it can be argued that in effect all countries in this system are paying some form of tribute to the USA. While in the 1980s it was Japan that led this process from Asia, it has now been joined by China.

As Hung (2016: 125) suggests:

> Asia's massive investment in low yield US Treasury bonds was tantamount to a tribute payment through which Asian savings were transformed into American's consumption power, prolonging US prosperity but creating a financial bubble in the 1980s and beyond.

Furthermore, in the period before the financial crisis there was a massive accumulation of US Treasury bonds, by both Asian (including China) and Middle Eastern countries. From 2003 to 2007, this increased by as much as

23% (Panitch and Gindin 2012: 309; Bernanke et al. 2011). There was also a massive increase—of 231%—in the purchase of Mortgage Backed Securities (MBSs) in the same period (Panitch and Gindin 2012: 309), the same MBSs that were central to the financial crisis when their values collapsed.

It was the crisis of 2007–08 and beyond that in many (but not all) ways undermined this virtuous (if unequal) circle. While cheap imports and debt helped to sustain demand in the USA, in the context of stagnant real wages this was bound to reach its limits at some point. The rising housing market was a major source of debt-led expansion, but for this to continue to expand, there needed to be an ever growing supply of new homeowners. The US home ownership peaked in 2004, and the subprime expansion can be seen as a desperate attempt to keep the mortgage market booming in this unfavourable context (Schwartz 2009: 189; JCHS 2008: 33). At the other end of the virtuous cycle, China's growth financed its own development efforts, including heavy investment in infrastructure. This had the effect of increasing raw material prices (see below), but also led to inflationary pressures, to which the Federal Reserve responded by increasing interest rates from 2004 through to 2006. Alongside the other pressures on the housing market, the increase in interest and therefore mortgage rates further undermined the conditions that supported the boom. This of course was exacerbated enormously by the spill-over of housing market problems into the rest of the economy, due to the securitisation of financial products and creation of all kinds of complex financial instruments.

For our purposes then, the mutual interdependence that characterised US–Chinese economic relations was undermined by the crash. The contraction in demand and fall in world trade led to a significant fall in exports and increase in unemployment in the months that immediately followed the crash. Some Chinese Communist Party officials suggested that this new situation presented an opportunity for China, through which it could shift from its dependence on export-led growth to a growth model which increasingly served the domestic market. The immediate response to the crisis was a massive fiscal stimulus package, amounting to $600 billion in 2008, a figure equivalent of 13% of GDP for that year, and which was seen as central to the development of a new growth model. Moreover, given that this stimulus relied on primary commodity imports, it served to revive falling commodity prices, thus reinforcing the idea that China was a friend of the global South. It is also a central factor in the argument that the South has decoupled from the North, as we will see.

### *The Commodity Supercycle and the Question of Decoupling*

The share of South–South trade in world trade increased from 9.9% in 2000–01, to 14.5% in 2006–07, to as much as 16.9% in 2009 (ADB 2011). While there are some problems with measuring such trade, what is important is that many parts of the South did indeed benefit from trade with the rest of the South, and specifically benefited from higher commodity prices. This is very important as a counter to the premature deindustrialisation argument outlined in Chap. 2. This primary commodities boom could be "viewed as a new super-cycle (i.e. a trend rise in real prices of a broad range of commodities that lasts for one to two decades and is driven by urbanization and industrialization in at least one major economy)" (UNCTAD 2012: 12). Therefore, this boom might be regarded as representing a shift away from the idea that there is a tendency for the terms of trade to decline for primary goods. It also therefore challenges the old development orthodoxy that in order to develop one must industrialise (see Chap. 2). Moreover, some manufacturing goods have seen a decline in their terms of trade in recent years, largely as a result of rising demand from China pushing up the prices of some primary commodities, alongside financial speculation in these markets (Farooki and Kaplinsky 2012: 180–6). This might suggest that specialisation in primary commodities is a useful strategy for at least some developing countries.

It is undoubtedly true that from around 2003, commodity prices started to rise substantially. Developing countries with a high share of oil and mineral and mining products in their total merchandise exports saw a substantial improvement in their terms of trade, and those with high fuel exports saw their terms of trade double from 2002 to 2011 (UNCTAD 2012: 8). This had a number of favourable spin-offs. For example, in 2000, average central government deficits in the South stood at around 3.5% of GDP but by 2006–07, this figure had declined to 0.5% (Akyuz 2012: 20). The real prices of energy and metals more than doubled from 2003 to 2008, and food increased by 75% (UNCTAD 2012: 9). In the first half of 2008, crude petroleum and food prices rose by more than 50% (UNCTAD 2012: 8–10). Alongside previous structural adjustment programmes in the 1980s and 1990s, this development reinforced the reversal of pro-industrialisation policies that had dominated development strategies in developing countries from the 1950s to the 1970s, including in some BRIC countries. Thus in Brazil from 1990 to 2005, Brazilian land allocated for soybean cultivation doubled, and China accounted for over 40% of its export market for this product in this period (Gallagher and Porzecanski 2010: 31–2). In the period from 2000 to 2006, Latin America's total export of copper increased by 237.5%, most of this accounted for by the Chinese market (Gallagher and Porzecanski 2010: 22).

There were significant reversals in the immediate aftermath of the financial crisis but there was then a period of recovery. China's stimulus package was central to the revival because the property and investment boom that followed had a high commodity import content (UNCTAD 2012: 12–13), and so commodity prices were 75% higher in 2010 than they had been in 2007 (Akyuz 2012: 36–7). China's primary commodity imports doubled in the period from 2009 to 2011, compared to a 50% increase for manufacturing imports (Akyuz 2014: 15). This significantly altered trading patterns in the post-2008 world. Thus, in 2007 Brazilian exports to the EU and the USA were four times and twice the level of its exports to China, respectively. By 2014, Brazilian exports to China and Europe were on a similar level and same and Brazilian exports to the USA were only around 50% of the value of its exports to China (Akyuz 2014: 15). For some writers, this represents a transformation of the international order in which China becomes less dependent on exports, while its focus on domestic consumption will lead to demand for Southern exports, thus facilitating an ongoing commodity supercycle (Kaplinsky and Farooki 2010), and a new international order in which the South is less dependent on the North, and in which the growth engine of China worked in favourable ways for other developing countries.

This section has outlined the specific international context which facilitated the rise of the South from around 2002 onwards. This was led by China, whose rise was in part facilitated by the foreign investment boom that started in the early 1990s, and after a brief slowdown in 2001, continued from 2002 onwards. This in turn led to an increase in annual deficits in the USA and an increase in the purchase of US Treasury securities, as well as heavy involvement in the US housing market, particularly the secondary mortgage market. These two factors then were central parts of our story, namely, the rise of China and the alleged decline of the USA. The third component was the rise of the rest of the South, which benefited from favourable spin-offs from the global North in terms of foreign investment (especially in Asian manufacturing) and from China's demands for primary commodities, which led to high commodity prices or what some have called a new commodity supercycle. Much of this context was undermined by the financial crisis of 2008, but from 2010 onwards, the South recovered rapidly. As the figures in Tables 2.1 and 2.2 demonstrate, world growth in 2010 was 4.1 %, with the developed world accounting for 2.6 % and the developing world 7.8 %, while in 2011 the corresponding figures were 2.8 % (world), 1.8 % (developed world) and 6 % (developing world). All four of the BRICs experienced rapid growth in 2010 with Russia growing at 4.8 %, India 10.4 %, China 10.3 % and Brazil 7.5 %. Central to recovery were significant stimulus programmes in each country, but especially in China, which had the effect of stimulating commodity prices, after they fell substantially in the immediate aftermath of the 2008 crisis. Thus, in the short term at least, the 2008 financial crisis actually reinforced the BRICs and rising South discourse (OECD 2010a, b; O' Neill 2013; UNDP 2013). Much of the argument already made in previous chapters has suggested that this argument is unconvincing, but, in tracing the shift from an emerging markets boom to emerging markets crisis, the next section argues that it now looks even more misguided.

## The Emerging Markets Crisis

This section examines in some depth how the international context which favoured the boom is now eventually giving rise to one that looks increasingly like an emerging markets bust. We have already seen how the international context that favoured the boom was in effect severed by the financial crisis, but we also saw how the developing world rapidly recovered from the crisis, especially when compared to the global North. Much of this was explained by successful stimulus policies, above all in China, which restored rapid growth there but also had positive spin-offs in the rest of the South. This section therefore follows a similar, though not identical structure to the previous one, to show how boom gave rise to bust. It first looks at China, then commodity prices, and then adds a separate section on decoupling which focuses less on South–South trade and more on capital flows.

### *China's Slowdown*

As we saw above, much of the focus in post-crisis China is the extent to which it has shifted from a policy based on export dependence to one based on boosting the domestic market. The stimulus programme that followed the crisis was thus seen as the start of a substantial shift in direction on the part of Chinese Communist Party elites. However, in fact the programme was actually quite limited in terms of its attempts to expand the domestic market. Only 20% of the package was actually allocated to social spending, and most of the rest went into investment in fixed assets, some of which already suffered from overcapacity (Caijing 2009). By 2009, China's fixed asset investment rate had reached 45% of GDP, and by 2010 the figure was 48.2%, compared to peaks in Taiwan and South Korea of 25–35% in the 1970s (Hung 2011: 221; Akyuz 2012: 23). As much as 80% of the growth in 2009 was due to investment (Akyuz 2012: 36). The problem then for China was that the stimulus was actually boosting investment rather more than consumption and this was bound to lead to overinvestment. Exports could in theory take up the slack but not in a changed international context of slower increases in demand for Chinese exports.

Significantly, the Chinese central bank increased its purchase of US Treasury bonds, from $618 billion in September 2008 to $1160 billion in December 2010 (Hung 2011: 234), and although increased purchases slowed down slightly in 2012, by September 2013 the figure had reached $1293 billion (US Treasury 2013). A small shift saw the figure down to $1271 billion by June 2015, but this was still over double the figure in September 2008 (US Treasury 2015). Most tellingly, when private investors have moved away from the purchase of such bonds, official sources have stepped in to fill the gap, most notably in the crisis period, when the proportion of US foreign debt held by official sources increased from 16.6% in January to June 2007, to 35.4% from January to June 2008 (Thompson 2010: 106). In the period from March 2007 to November 2014, total foreign holdings of US Treasury securities increased from $2 trillion to $6 trillion, of which $4.1 trillion were held by official sources (US Treasury 2015). At the same time, while the US trade deficit increased at a slower rate in the aftermath of the financial crisis, reaching $273 billion by 2010 compared to $268 billion in 2008, it has since increased again, albeit at a slower rate than in the period from 2000 to 2008, so that by 2012, the deficit was $315 billion, by 2013, $318 billion; and by 2014, $342 billion (US Census Bureau 2015). The Chinese currency devaluations of August 2015 (Inman 2015) may also reflect a continued commitment to an export-led strategy, even as the pre-2008 international context no longer exists. This suggests a picture of China continuing to pursue an export-led strategy, albeit in a far less favourable international environment, where US import growth from China has slowed (see Table 4.1) rather than simply radically shifting its priorities to focusing on the domestic market.

**Table 4.1** US imports from China, in US $million, selected years. *Source*: adapted from US Census Bureau 2015

| *1990* | *1995* | *2000* | *2002* | *2004* | *2006* | *2008* | *2010* | *2012* | *2013* | *2014* |
|---|---|---|---|---|---|---|---|---|---|---|
| 15237 | 45543 | 100018 | 125193 | 196682 | 287774 | 337773 | 364953 | 425626 | 440447 | 466656 |

In other words, in the five years since the outbreak of the financial crisis, Chinese purchases have soared. It bears repeating that China's role in the world economy has increasingly been one of manufacturing in the context of the development of global commodity chains, in which it is not a leader in any major sector within such networks.

China thus faces serious difficulties in the years ahead. This is not simply a question of shifting away from export dependence to focus more on the domestic market, or the related question of overcoming the middle income trap, under which a country may face competitive pressures from technological leaders above it, and cheaper labour producers below it. Indeed, by the first quarter of 2015, credit growth and GDP growth had returned to levels similar to that of early 2009, when China was most immediately and directly affected by the financial crisis (Lopez 2015), and by July and August 2015 there were considerable concerns about the futures of China's development strategy, reflected in increasingly volatile stock markets. The current debate about China rebalancing is essentially an argument about China's attempt to shift to a greater focus on domestic consumption, and to upgrade from lower-value production (as part of the global production networks discussed in earlier chapters) to the higher-value production and services primarily serving the home market. However, China has a longer-term problem of overcapacity which predates the financial crisis, in which growth has been led by exports or investment more than consumption (Hung 2016: 155). This is exacerbated by competition between different localities, so that there are in effect 32 "developmental states" rather than one, or expanding investment and attempting to increase exports. There is also the related problem of enormous debt and the question of non-performing loans, which means that in effect many banks and companies are bankrupt. They are kept afloat by state revenue, much of which comes from foreign exchange generated by exports; in 1999, the state bailed out banks and state-owned enterprises through absorbing approximately 2 trillion RMB of non-performing loans (Hung 2016: 157). This means that "(w)henever economic crisis is deferred, China becomes ever more dependent on its export sector to divert the overcapacity problem in the domestic economy" (Hung 2016: 158). We have already seen that 2009 saw a sharp fall in exports and since 2010 year on year export growth has not been as fast as it was before 2008. This was where the stimulus was important but, for all the short-term growth in China and favourable spin-offs for commodity exporters, the problem remains that the stimulus has only exacerbated longer-term problems. In the period after 2009, fixed asset investment growth has outstripped GDP growth rates. Thus, while the export share of GDP peaked at 40 % in 2006, and then fell to less than 30 % by 2009, by 2012 it still remained as high as 28 %, even in the context of unfavourable world market conditions. The household consumption share of GDP peaked at around 45 % in 1999, and since then has fallen to 37 % in 2008, around 38 % in 2009, and had been hovering between 36 % and 39 % from 2010 to 2012. This is much lower than in 1999 despite the 2009 stimulus. Most tellingly, gross fixed capital formation as a percentage of GDP increased from 39 % in 2007 to 48 % in 2012 (Hung 2016: 162). Local governments have invested heavily in new building, new roads, airports, even new towns and giant shopping malls, but many of these have limited demand. The South China Morning Post thus recently reported on the case of the newly rebuilt airport at Dachangshan island, off the north–east coast, which was based on a planned 42,000 annual passengers by 2010 and 78,000 by 2015. In 2013, only 4000 passengers passed through the airport (Hart-Landsberg 2015). The problems of overcapacity and debt have therefore not gone away and have in fact worsened. With the loosening of bank lending after 2009, local government and local enterprises have accumulated debt more than three times the value of the fiscal stimulus, a figures of around $2 trillion. Standard Chartered Bank estimated in mid-2014 that the total outstanding debt in the Chinese economy reached 251 % of GDP, and possibly as much as 282 % in early 2015, compared to 147 % in 2008 (Hung 2016: 160, 163). At the time of writing, the serious stock market volatility which plagued the Chinese economy in the summer of 2015 appeared not to be over. In August 2015 the yuan was devalued—possibly as part of another export drive, or possibly as part of an attempt to increase liquidity and thus consumption, but actually leading to capital export on a massive scale (even in the context of continued limits on the movement of capital). Whatever explanation is more convincing, both point to serious weaknesses in the Chinese economy. Similarly, in the period from November 2014 to early 2016 there were six interest rate cuts which attempted to boost economic activity (Allen 2016).

### *The End of the Commodity Supercycle*

As we saw above, much of the argument concerning the rise of the South, especially after the financial crisis, rests on the idea that the commodity supercycle will continue for a substantial period of time, as China's development strategy draws on demand for commodities from the rest of the South (Farooki and Kaplinsky 2012). The implication that follows is that there is far less need for developing countries to industrialise to avoid unequal terms of trade, and indeed the premature deindustrialisation identified by Rodrik (2015) actually does not matter (see Chap. 2). This argument was always problematic in terms of longer-term questions of development, for as Table 4.2 makes clear, commodity price increases have slowed down and in some respects have now been reversed. In 2013 and 2014, most commodity prices fell from their peak in 2011. It is true that commodity prices in the period from 2012 to 2014 were on average at higher levels than they were in the period from 2003 to 2008, but for high growth rates to persist for the developing world as a whole, primary commodity prices will need to increase, not stabilise or decrease. Recent patterns are not promising to say the least, with significant falls in commodity prices, including in oil, which at the time of writing (January 2016) has fallen to below $30 a barrel. Copper prices fell by 14% in 2014, and by as much as 10% in the first two weeks of January 2015 (Pratley 2015). Crude oil prices fell by 21.3% in December 2014 and 21.6% in January 2015 (IMF 2015a: 1), while metal prices fell by 4.9% and 5.7% in the same months (IMF 2015a: 2). In the first six months of 2015, commodity prices as a whole fell by 5.8% (IMF 2015c: 1). While these are only a brief snapshot of trends, complicated further by speculative practices in global financial markets, when examined next to annual trends since 2012 (see Table 4.2, they do tend to point to a picture of commodity price falls and certainly the end of the commodity supercycle. Indeed,

**Table 4.2** World primary commodity prices, excluding petroleum, 2008–14 (percentage change from previous year), adapted from UNCTAD 2015: 12)

| | *2009* | *2010* | *2011* | *2012* | *2013* | *2014* | *2015* |
|---|---|---|---|---|---|---|---|
| All commodities except petroleum | -16.9 | 20.4 | 17.9 | -8.3 | -6.7 | -6.1 | -13.1 |
| All food | -8.5 | 7.4 | 17.8 | -1.4 | -7.4 | -4.1 | -12.2 |
| Copper | -26.3 | 47 | 17.1 | -9.9 | -7.8 | -6.4 | -13.5 |

the International Monetary Fund (IMF) commodity price index, which measures the prices of all commodities, shows a sharp fall in prices from a post-crisis peak of 210 in the first quarter of 2011, down to a figure of less than 125 in January 2015 (IMF 2015b). Similarly, Table 4.2 shows a clear downward trend in commodity prices since 2012, and if anything, a sharpening of such a decline in 2015.

We might add two further points which further undermine the argument that the commodity supercycle presents an opportunity for all in the developing world. First, rather than representing an opportunity for all countries in the South, the impact of high commodity prices will vary according to whether or not developing countries are net commodity importers. Thus, Jenkins (2011: 84) suggests that in Latin America, El Salvador, Nicaragua, Costa Rica, Panama and Uruguay have all been losers in recent years. Second, as already argued (Chap. 2), concentration on primary commodity production does not lead to the linkages and high productivity that specialisation in some manufacturing production can generate (Chang 2012), and this argument becomes even more forceful once commodity prices stabilise or fall, for it leaves those dependent on this strategy vulnerable to price falls. This is precisely what is happening in the international economy now and is central to the shift from boom to bust. It appear then that the old development argument in favour of industrialisation—and thus also Rodrik's arguments concerning premature industrialisation—retains its force. To therefore make claims for a rising South when much of it (including Brazil, one of the BRICs) has deindustrialised, and therefore exposed to falling commodity prices, is misguided.

### *The Myth of the Decoupling Thesis and Reality of Slowdown in the South*

In the last section, we also saw that some of the claims made for a rising South rest on the claim that it is no longer dependent on or indeed has decoupled from the global North. This in turn rests on the rise of South–South trade, part of which is the rise in primary commodity prices and the fact that China has become a major engine of the world economy. However, much of the argument around decoupling underestimates the centrality of capital flows to the South, much of which originate from the global North. Indeed, one of the reasons for the recovery in the South from 2010 onwards was precisely these flows. Thus in 2013, private capital flows to the South totalled around $1.3 trillion, slightly higher than the pre-crisis peak of $1.2 trillion in 2007 (IIF 2015a).

Dependence on capital flows is not necessarily undesirable, and as we have seen the USA is dependent on capital flows to finance accumulating debt obligations (even if, as we have also seen, it pays low rates of interest on such debt). There are, however, some potential problems with certain kinds of flows to the South, and these are now in fact being realised and are a central component of the shift from boom to bust. In terms of a breakdown of flows, more mobile equity flows to the South stood at $659 billion in 2013 (up from $566 million in 2007) while portfolio investment increased sharply after the crisis (up from $77 billion in 2007 to $148 billion in 2009) before falling back to $77 billion in 2013. Less mobile FDI stood at $488 billion in 2007 and after falling down to $387 billion in 2009 recovered to $590 billion in 2011 and then fell back to $535 billion in 2012 (IIF 2015a). What is particularly important for our purposes is what has happened and is happening to the more mobile forms of capital flows, for from late 2014 onwards there has been a substantial shift and net capital outflows are now more significant than inflows.

Particularly important here is to understand the link between economic policy in the developed world and capital flows to the global South. After a brief period of fiscal stimulus, the dominant response of the advanced capitalist countries to the crisis was to focus on monetary policy, and in particular to promote quantitative easing (QE). The rationale for such a policy was to recapitalise banks so that they could then lend to business and households, and thus stimulate economic activity. While it is likely that this policy prevented a deeper recession, lending to businesses and households has been quite low. Much of the money has ended up back in central banks as excess reserves but there has also been some investment at "the riskier end of the credit spectrum" such as in high yield bonds (BIS 2013), leading to a boom in equities. This is not just the case in the US stock market, but also in stock markets in the global South. The recovery and rise of equity investment (and volatility of portfolio investment) therefore is in part a product of QE policies in the North. Thus it is not only the case that equity and portfolio investment is more mobile than FDI, and thus can easily be removed from a country, it is also that this is linked to a very specific policy developed in the global North in response to the financial crisis, and one which will eventually end. Indeed, in May and June 2013, the Federal Reserve hinted at the beginning of the end of QE, which led to a ten-year high in Treasury bond yields (Akyuz

2014: 18). That this was followed by a partial postponement of large reductions in QE, the effects in the summer of 2013, and again at the end that year, were significant and a possible sign of more serious effects to follow. From June to August 2013, investors withdrew $64 billion from developing country mutual funds, and there were sharp sell-offs in equity, bond and currency markets (Ghosh 2014). In January 2014, a number of countries, including South Africa, Turkey, and Argentina, faced the prospect of currency crises, leading some to conclude that at the start of 2014, "the financial gurus looked into their crystal balls and said that for the first time since the crash of 2008 they were more worried about emerging markets than the dull old west" (Elliot 2014). Thus, while in the period before the financial crisis and from 2009 onwards, net private inflows to emerging markets exceeded outflows (with a positive "surplus" of $417 billion in 2010), this situation was in effect reversed as net capital outflows exceeded inflows by $98 billion in 2013 and by as much as $299 billion in 2014 (IIF 2015b: 3–4). While this last figure was later amended to $111 billion, the figure for 2015 has been said to be as high as $735 billion, much of this dominated by outflows from China (IIF 2016). This is a period of enormous volatility; for instance, from June 2014 to July 2015, total net capital outflows for the 19 largest "emerging markets" reached $940 billion, almost double the net outflow in the first three quarters that followed the financial crisis in 2008–2009 (Kynge and Wheatley 2015).

Longer-term direct foreign investment from China is unlikely to compensate for these trends. Indeed, Chinese greenfield and expansionary FDI in Africa in the first half of 2015 fell by as much as 84% compared to the same period a year earlier (Klasa 2015). Moreover, most of this investment was in raw materials, China's original interest in the continent. While the 84% fall is distorted somewhat by the surge in investment in 2014, it remains the case that following a peak of $11.7 billion in 2008, it was followed by an average annual total of $1.5 billion for each of the five years that followed (Klasa 2015). It is true, as Chap. 2 argued, that trade has been more significant than investment in Chinese–African relations, but in value terms this faces the problem of falling commodity prices as discussed above. Moreover, FDI does reflect broader trends on the world economy, and capital inflows (from all countries) as a share of GDP in the South fell from around 8% in 2007 to 2% in 2015 (Klasa 2015). This is particularly problematic when combined with the likely capital outflow figures, discussed above.

Whatever the precise figures may be, it is clear that alongside a reversal of capital inflows to the South, a run on currencies, falling current account surpluses and increasing deficits, this is the start of a sharp reversal in the fortunes of the South. As previous financial crisis in the South have shown, a policy of rapid capital inflows can have the effect of increasing the value of national currencies, thus making imports cheaper and undermining a domestic productive basis—what Saad-Filho (2010) has called "production substitution." While in 2008 total capital inflows to developing countries were about $20 billion, by 2010 the figure was $600 billion. However, fixed investment growth in developing countries actually *slowed* in the post-crisis period, so little of this money was used for productive purposes (Stiglitz 2016). Once again then, we see how premature deindustrialisation undermines the prospects for much of the South once mobile capital inflows become net outflows, especially when combined with falling commodity prices. Indeed, Finance Ministers in South Africa and Brazil have recently complained that they are caught in the crossfire in an effective currency war between the European Central Bank and the Federal Reserve, as capital inflows put upward pressure on their currencies and fuel a speculative and consumer boom (Marcus 2012). Meanwhile, while the former chief economist of one investment bank identified the BRICs (O' Neill 2001), and then the MINT (Mexico, Indonesia, Nigeria and Turkey) countries (O'Neill 2014), another investment bank identified five fragile emerging economies (Lord 2013), four of which are either BRIC or MINT countries (Brazil, India, Turkey and Indonesia) and the fifth (South Africa) of which is the new addition to the BRICS. The shift from net inflows to outflows is a dangerous one which could have devastating effects for countries in the South, even as some of them make some attempt to diversify their productive base and (in surplus countries) build up foreign exchange reserves to protect their currency in the face of such a crisis. Whatever the future holds, this is clearly not a situation in which the global South has decoupled from the global North.

Thus, there is the slowdown in growth in the world and in the global South, as seen by the growth figures for 2015. At the time of writing (February 2016) it appears that the world grew by 2.5% in 2015, with developed countries seeing an annual growth increase of 1.9%, while the developing world saw an increase of 4.1% (UNCTAD 2015: 3). On the face of it, this is not a particularly sharp decline from the previous three years growth figures in the South (4.7%, 4.8% and 4.5%) though it is significantly less than the 2011 figure of 6% (UNCTAD 2015: 3; and see Table 2.2 in Chap. 2). But, on the other hand, there are significant regional differences. Africa's growth rate of 3.2% is significantly lower than in the period before 2008 and after 2010, but most marked is the downturn in Latin America, which barely saw any growth at all. Even more significant, Brazil's slowdown in growth rates meant that for 2015, growth was actually negative at –0.2% (UNCTAD 2015: 3). This compares with growth rates of 5.2% in 2011, 2.8% in 2012, 3.3% in 2013 and 0.8% in 2014. In 2007, Brazil's growth rate was 6%. This fall in growth rates and shift into negative territory represents Brazil's biggest slump since 1901, beating even the rate of contraction that followed the 1982 debt crisis (Watts 2016). China remains an important motor of the world economy, but its official growth rates (and some have suggested the real rates are considerably lower) have significantly slowed, from 14.2% in 2007, and 9.6% in 2008, 9.2% in 2009, and 10.4% in 2010 (when the stimulus was most effective), down to 9.3% in 2011, 7.7% in both 2012 and 2013, 7.4% in 2014, and 6.9% in 2015 (UNCTAD 2015: 12). Russia's boom both before 2008 and immediately after 2010 has also ended, with much slower growth rates in 2013 (just above 1%) and 2014 (below 1%) and negative growth of over -3% in 2015 (Trading Economics 2016). India bucks this trend, with continued high rates of growth but it is not sufficiently linked to other countries in the South to act as an engine of growth in the way that China has, particularly since the financial crisis.

## Conclusion

One of the most interesting arguments currently (in January 2016) being deployed in the West is that if there is a slowdown in the world economy, then this is China's fault because it has not adopted the correct policies and needs to reform in more market friendly ways. This is an odd argument as it is often made—or at least implied—by those same people (like British Chancellor of the Exchequer George Osborne) who previously suggested that China's success story was due to its embrace of market friendly policies. This argument overestimates the degree of China's previous rise, but also serves to remind us that the Western world has hardly made a full recovery from the 2008 crisis. This is an important point, not least for the wider argument of the book, for in suggesting that the rise of the South has been exaggerated, and that we appear to be shifting towards an emerging markets crisis, I am not suggesting that all is well in the developed economies. Far from it. But what I am suggesting is that it is mistaken to see the rise of the South and the fall of the USA and the West as a zero-sum game, and rather, as I have argued in more detail elsewhere (Kiely 2015), the US crisis is a global crisis, and is therefore a problem for the South as well as the West or global North. Much of the recovery in the global North is predicated on renewed asset bubbles, which in turn are linked to the ways in which China remains incorporated into the liberal international order. This suggests then that the West's problems are also China's problems and vice versa.

It also suggests that the idea that the BRICs and the South had decoupled from the global North after the financial crisis, and especially from 2010 onwards, was mistaken. An emerging markets crisis is now unravelling and this reflects not only the continued weaknesses and dependency of the South in the global economy, but also the unfolding of those specific international conditions that facilitated the emerging markets boom in the first place. In particular, China's growth remains export and investment dependent, and there are serious long-term problems in the Chinese economy. In particular, China continues to purchase US debt, and this is linked to the continued importance of its export strategy. This allows China to generate massive foreign exchange reserves, part of which have been used to bail out debtors in the domestic economy. Since the financial crisis, the purchase of US debt continues, but the capacity to continue massive export growth and foreign exchange reserves has been undermined. Bailouts can continue but over time they will become less likely not least because debt continues to grow alongside massive overcapacity, a situation exacerbated by the fiscal stimulus introduced in response to the crisis. Thus, the recovery after 2010 masked these problems but at the costs of continued overcapacity and debt, and less room for manoeuvre in terms of the revenue generated by exports being used to bail out debtors. Given that much of the rest of the South, including the BRICs, has emerged because of China's continued expansion, China's slowdown and economic problems are also serious problems for the rest of the South. For the global North, the extent of reliance on the Chinese market for its own exports has been exaggerated, not least because this is often linked to the spurious rising South thesis (Chang 2016). On the other hand, China is an important source of cheap imports and debt financing, and some Western banks have heavy exposure to the Chinese economy. In this respect China's problems will impact on the global North as well as the South, but the uneven impact that is likely to occur also reflects the South's continued subordinate place in the global order.

## References

ADB. 2011. *Asian Development Outlook*. Manila: Asian Development Bank.

Akyuz, Y. 2012. The Staggering Rise of the South? South Centre Research Paper no. 44, Geneva, pp. 1–54.

Akyuz, Y. 2014. Crisis Management in the United States and Europe: Impact on Developing Countries and Longer Term Consequences. South Centre Research Paper no. 50, Geneva, pp. 1–41.

Allen, K. 2016. Global Economic Turmoil to Dominate Davos Discussions. *The Guardian*, January 17. http://www.theguardian.com/business/2016/jan/17/global-economic-turmoil-dominate-davos. Accessed 17 Jan 2016.

Bernanke, B., C. Bertaut, L. Pounder DeMarco, and S. Kamin. 2011. International Capital Flows and the Returns to Safe Assets in the United States, 2003-2007. International Finance Discussion Paper no. 1014, Washington, pp. 1–35.

BIS. 2013. International Banking and Financial Market Development. *Quarterly Review*, September. http://www.bis.org/publ/qtrpdf/r_qt1309.htm. Accessed 8 Jan 2015.

Caijing. 2009. Severe Unemployment Jeopordizes Labor Contract Law. July 16. http://english.caijing.com.cn. Accessed 4 Mar 2012.

Chang, H-J. 2012. Africa Needs an Active Industrial Policy to Sustain Its Growth. http://www.theguardian.com/commentisfree/2012/jul/15/africa-industrial-policy-washington-orthodoxy. Accessed 5 Mar 2015.

Chang, H-J. 2016. Don't Blame China for These Economic Jitters. *The Guardian*, January 21. http://www.theguardian.com/commentisfree/2016/jan/21/dont-blame-china-global-west-economic-recovery-asset-bubbles. Accessed 21 Jan 2016.

Dicken, P. 2011. *Global Shift*. 6th ed. London: Sage.

Dooley, M., D. Folkerts-Landau, and P. Garber. 2009. Bretton Woods II Still Defines the International Monetary System. *Pacific Economic Review* 13(3): 297–311.

Elliot, L. 2014. Emerging Markets Crisis Is History Repeating Itself. *The Guardian*, February 4.

Farooki, M. and R. Kaplinsky (2012) *The Impact of China on Global Commodity Prices* (London: Routledge).

Gallagher, K., and R. Porzecanski. 2010. *The Dragon in the Room*. Stanford: Stanford University Press.

Ghosh, J. 2014. Emerging Markets: Déjà vu All over Again. http://triplecrisis.com/emerging-markets-deja-vu-all-over-again/. Accessed 5 Mar 2015.

Hart-Landsberg, M. 2015. Signs of Global Slowdown. http://blogs.lclark.edu/hart-landsberg/category/china/. Accessed 14 Jan 2016.

Hung, H.F. (2009) 'America's Head Servant', *New Left Review* II/64: 97–108.

Hung, H.F. 2011. Sinomania: Global Crisis, China's Crisis? In *The Socialist Register 2012*, eds. L. Panitch, C. Leys and G. Albo, 217–234. London: Merlin.

Hung, H.F. 2016. *The China Boom: Why China Will Not Rule the World*. Cambridge: Harvard University Press.

IIF. 2015a. Aggregate Capital Flows Data. https://www.iif.com/publications/capital-flows. Accessed 5 Mar 2015.

IIF. 2015b. Capital Flows to Emerging Markets (Jan. 14, 2015, Washington: IIF, 1–36).

IIF. 2016. 'Capital Flows to Emerging Markets' (Washington, IIF), pp.1–36.

IMF. 2015a. Commodity Market Monthly. February 11, 2015. http://www.imf.org/external/np/res/commod/pdf/monthly/020115.pdf. Accessed 5 Mar 2015.

IMF. 2015b. IMF Commodity Price Indices. http://www.imf.org/external/np/res/commod/images/chart_lg.jpg. Accessed 5 Mar 2015.

IMF. 2015c. IMF Commodity Price Indices. http://www.imf.org/external/np/res/commod/pdf/monthly/071615.pdf. Accessed 7 Sept 2015.

Inman, P. 2015. China Ends Three Fays of Yuan Devaluation. http://www.theguardian.com/business/2015/aug/14/china-halts-yuan-devaluation-with-slight-official-rise-against-us-dollar. Accessed 7 Sept 2015.

JCHS. 2008. *The State of the Nation's Housing*. Cambridge: Harvard Joint Center for Housing Studies.

Jenkins, R. 2011. The "China Effect" on Global Commodity Prices and Latin American Export Earnings. *CEPAL Review* 103: 73–87.

Kaplinsky, R., and M. Farooki. 2010. *The Impact of China on Global Commodity Prices: The Global Reshaping of the Resource Sector*. London: Routledge.

Kiely, R. 2015. *The BRICs, US 'Decline' and Global Transformations*. London: Palgrave.

Klasa, A. 2015. Chinese Investment in Africa Plunges 83%. *Financial Times*, October 21.

Kynge, J., and J. Wheatley. 2015. Emerging Markets: Fixing a Broken Model. *Financial Times*, August 31.

Lopez, L. 2015. 'Hard Landing', 'Business Insider'. April 15, 2015. http://uk.businessinsider.com/china-charts-look-like-2009-again-2015-4?r=US. Accessed 24 Apr 2015.

Lord, J. 2013. EM Currencies: The Fragile Five. http://www.morganstanleyfa.com/public/projectfiles/dce4d168-15f9-4245-9605-e37e2caf114c.pdf. Accessed 16 Feb 2015.

Marcus, G. 2012. Consider the Small Nations Caught in the Central Bank Crossfire. *Financial Times*, May 3.

OECD. 2010a. *Perspectives on Global Development, 2010, Shifting Wealth*. Paris: OECD Development Centre.

OECD. 2010b. Perspectives of Global Development, 2010, Shifting Wealth: Summary. http://www.oecd.org/dev/pgd/45451514.pdf. Accessed 26 Jan 2013.

O' Neill, J. 2001. Building Better Global Economic BRICs. Goldman Sachs Global Economics Paper no. 66, pp. 1–16.
O' Neill, J. 2013. *The Growth Map*. London: Portfolio Penguin.
O'Neill, J. 2014. The MINT Countries: The Next Economic Giants. http://www.bbc.co.uk/news/magazine-25548060. Accessed 28 Feb 2014.
Panitch, L., and S. Gindin. 2012. *The Making of Global Capitalism*. London: Verso.
Pratley, N. 2015. Copper No Longer a Safe Haven as Big Miners Suffer Rocky Commodity Prices. http://www.theguardian.com/business/blog/2015/jan/14/copper-commodity-fall-prices-big-miners-glencore?CMP=share_btn_link. Accessed 5 Mar 2015.
Rodrik, D. 2015. *Premature Deindustrialization*. Cambridge: Harvard University, unpublished paper.
Saad-Filho, A. 2010. Neoliberalism, Democracy and Development Policy in Brazil. *Development and Society* 39(1): 1–28.
Schwartz, H. 2009. Origins and Consequences of the US Subprime Crisis. In *The Politics of Housing Booms and Busts*, eds. H. Schwartz and L. Seabrooke, 188–207. Basingstoke: Palgrave.
Stiglitz, J. (2016) 'Closing the capital drain from emerging markets', *The Guardian*, January 19.
Steinfeld, E. 2010. *Playing Our Game*. Cambridge: Cambridge University Press.
Thompson, H. 2010. *China and the Mortgaging of America*. Basingstoke: Palgrave.
Trading Economics. 2016. Russia Growth Rates. http://www.tradingeconomics.com/russia/gdp-growth-annual. Accessed 15 Feb 2016.
UNCTAD. 2012. *Trade and Development Report 2012*. Geneva: UNCTAD.
UNCTAD. 2015. *World Investment Report 2015*. Geneva: UNCTAD.
UNDP. 2013. *Human Development Report 2013*. New York: UNDP.
US Census Bureau. 2015. Trade in Goods and Services with China. www.census.gov/foreign-trade/balance/c5700.html. Accessed 16 Feb 2015.
US Treasury Department. 2013. Major Foreign Holders of Treasury Securities. http://www.treasury.gov/ticdata/Publish/mfh.txt. Accessed 7 Mar 2014.
US Treasury Department. 2015. Major Foreign Holders of Treasury Securities. http://www.treasury.gov/ticdata/Publish/mfh.txt. Accessed 17 Feb 2015.
Watts, J. 2016. Zika Crisis and Economic Woes Bring Gloom to Brazil's Olympic Build Up. *The Guardian*, February 5. http://www.theguardian.com/world/2016/feb/05/brazil-faces-steep-hurdles-ahead-of-olympics-zika-and-economic-crisis. Accessed 5 Feb 2016.

CHAPTER 5

# Questioning the Rise of the South III: The Question of Global Inequality

**Abstract** This chapter adds weight to the previous arguments by focusing on the geography of global inequality and poverty. It briefly introduce questions around measuring inequality (between countries, within countries and between peoples across countries), and to some extent problematises these measures as well as upbeat assessments around poverty reduction (which are related to upbeat liberal internationalist assessments of the rise of the South). It then draws on the latest available data to examine questions of concentrations of global poverty and inequality in middle income countries—precisely those countries seen as part of the rise of the South. While optimists suggest that with growth, poverty will be reduced further, it will be shown that in fact the growth rates in middle income countries have had mixed results at best when it comes to poverty reduction, and that this is in part because of growing inequality within those countries. This discussion is once again related back to the modernisation and dependency debate.

**Keywords** Inequality • Poverty • Dependency

So far we have questioned the rising South and declining US theses by examining the following: hierarchies in the global economy through an examination of corporate ownership; the limits of the rise of the South via



R. Kiely, *The Rise and Fall of Emerging Powers*,
DOI 10.1007/978-3-319-34012-8_5

an examination of the international context which facilitated this rise, and how this context has now shifted to a less favourable one; and related to this, how this has given rise to a shift from an emerging markets boom to an emerging markets crisis, most visible in the years 2015 and early 2016. One possible objection to the argument about the emerging markets crisis discourse is that it focuses only on shorter-term issues rather than longer-term trends. This is precisely why we first examined the limits of the rise of the South in the context of the emerging markets boom discourse, as well as corporate ownership. But there is a further, longer-term issue which needs to be examined and further puts the rising South discourse into context. Furthermore, depending on how it is measured, it also can shift the focus from one of that concentrates on relations between states (in the context of an increasingly globalised capitalism), to one which can focus on relations between individuals, as we will see. This is the question of inequality.

The chapter examines this question first through a brief outline of different ways of measuring inequality, and how these are used to make claims about inequality in the world order. It then moves on to examine in more depth some current debates around inequality, particularly in the light of the data generated by the latest, 2011, International Price Comparison, the implications of which are still the subject, five years later, of considerable debate. Some of the latest data on inequality is then presented, which, it is fair to say, seriously undermines the rising South thesis. Given the shift from boom to crisis, some possible future scenarios are also briefly discussed.

## Inequality: International, National and Global

There are various measures of inequality in the international order. Perhaps most common is international inequality which measures inequality trends between countries, based on income. While in many ways a useful measure, not least for understanding trends in terms of the global North–South divide, on its own it has some limitations. The first reason for this is that it ignores population and so the measure should factor in inequality between countries on a per capita basis. One part of the rising South story is that it has eroded the trend from 1820 to 1950, in which much of the South witnessed declining shares of world GDP, and the small increase in shares after this date (27% in 1950, 28.5% by 1973), is then followed by a sharp increase to as much as 47.9% by 2010

(Nayyar 2009: 5; Akyuz 2012). However, this data ignores the fact that in this period population growth was much higher in the developing world, and when per capita GDP is factored in, we see a different picture. Based on per capita and constant market exchange rates, the South's share of global GDP per capita barely increases at all in the period from 1970 to 2005, increasing from just 4.7% in 1970 to 4.9% in 2005 (Nayyar 2013: 59–61). The second important consideration is regional diversity. Again based on market exchange rates, while the ratio of per capita GDP in Asia to that of the developed world shifted from 1:20 in 1970 to 1:11 in 2010, in Latin America it remained broadly the same (1:5) while in Africa it shifted from 1:12 to as much as 1:24 over the same period (Nayyar 2013: 59–61). For all the hyperbole about the rise of the South then, even the OECD (2010: 37) admits that "the convergence observed in the 2000s was not statistically significant."

Nonetheless, it does appear that from around the late 1980s to 2005s, there was a small decline in international inequality. More significant, since 2005, international inequality has fallen at a very significant rate, though the slowdown in the South from 2014 might now change things again. Nonetheless, from 2005 to around 2013, falling international inequality was significant enough to more than compensate for a second trend in the international order, which was rising inequality within countries, or national inequality (Chen and Ravallion 2012). This is considered in a moment but we should also note if China is excluded then in fact inequality between countries has actually risen in recent years (Edward and Sumner 2013: 14–15).

In terms of national inequality, the general trend has been one of greater inequality within countries in recent years (with Latin America and Brazil in particular countering this trend, but this is again likely to change with the shift from boom to bust). Thus, based on household income in 104 countries, inequality increased in 73 of these countries in this period and fell in only 24, with the rest remaining broadly the same (UNCTAD 2012: 57). In China, inequality has risen rapidly and the Gini coefficient measure of inequality (with zero at perfect equality and 1 at complete inequality) has risen from 0.28 in the early 1980s to 0.48 in 2008 (Nolan 2012: 69). It has been estimated that 0.1% of households have 45.8% of total household wealth—that is, 1.3 million people hold almost half of the household wealth of 1.3 billion people (Nolan 2012: 69). Moreover, while incomes might have risen, the financial burden of health care or education might have risen for some even more sharply, leading to less than impressive social development indicators (Reddy 2007)—which itself is a further reason for treating income-based measures of inequality with some degree of scepticism. From 1980 to 2010, life expectancy rose from 67.8 to 73.5, but this is actually around 50 % slower than other countries with similar life expectancy levels in 1980, even though these latter countries experienced much slower growth rates (Reddy 2007: 53).

These trends are also visible in the developed world. In Britain, the top 1 % income group increased its share of national income from 6 % in 1979 to 16 % in 2007, while in the USA, the equivalent figures were 8 % and 18 %. For the USA, if capital gains are included, then the figures are 8.5 % (1979) and 23.5 % (UNCTAD 2012: 49–50). Since 1980, the share of wages in GDP fell by 5 percentage points or more in Australia, Belgium, Finland, France, the Netherlands, Norway, Sweden, the UK and the USA, and by 10 points or more in Austria, Germany, Ireland, New Zealand and Portugal (UNCTAD 2012: 52).

We have seen then that there are two trends in the international order in terms of inequality. One is that international inequality—between countries—has fallen, while the other suggests that national inequality—within countries—has risen. And as already noted, this has had the positive impact of a small reduction in inequality between peoples irrespective of country. In other words, there has been a fall in global inequality, which is essentially inequality which factors in inequality both between and within countries. This upbeat story has also led optimistic claims concerning falling poverty headcounts, based on the number of people living above an absolute poverty benchmark of $1.25 a day. Thus, using this figure, the number of people living in absolute poverty has declined over recent years, with figures ranging from 1.8 billion (1990) to 1.37 billion (2005), 1.4 billion (1980) down to 1.2 billion or 1 billion (2008) and $982 billion by 2012 (Chen and M. Ravallion 2012; World Bank 2002: 30; Edward and Sumner 2015: 33). As a result, the proportion of the world's people living in extreme poverty fell from 43 % in 1990 to 22.4 % in 2008 (UNDP 2013: 12). The standard argument accounting for this decline echoes the liberal internationalist and neoliberal arguments outlined in Chap. 2, namely, that just as the South has risen, so too has poverty declined as a result of the embrace of market friendly policies by emerging markets (World Bank 2002). In the words of Jim O' Neill (2013: 232), "(g)lobalization may widen inequality within certain national borders, but on a global basis it has been a huge force for good, narrowing inequality among people on an unprecedented scale." In terms of our "framing devices," this suggests a story of convergence or modernisation.

## International Inequality: The Limits of the Rising South Thesis Revisited

So far then we have accepted some trends that conform to the rising South thesis, particularly around questions of poverty reduction and international and global inequality. We have also briefly noted some possible limitations to this thesis, around the question of China's influence over the general data, regional variation, on per capita measures. Here I want to develop these arguments further to shed new light on the relationship between the rising South thesis and wider trends in inequality, and reflect briefly on where future trends might be headed. It does so first by making some brief observations about absolute poverty before moving on to a much wider consideration of inequality trends, which explicitly relate these issues back to the modernisation/convergence versus dependency/divergence debate outlined in Chap. 2.

In terms of absolute poverty, this has been defined in recent years as referring to those living on less than $1.25 a day (though see below for possible changes), and this measure is adjusted in each specific country to take account of local purchasing power. Purchasing power parity (PPP) is measured through a system of international price comparisons (in 1985, 1993, 2005 and 2011) which are then adjusted to take account of annual changes to particular economies. This concept makes comparisons across regional variations in prices by constructing a basket of goods. On the face of it this is a sound principle because the value of the US dollar might be greater in one economy than it is in another, not least in the USA itself where living expenses might be higher than they are in a poorer country. The problem is that the content of the basket of goods by which comparisons are made might draw on inappropriate goods for measuring the extent on poverty. This was particularly problematic in the case of the 2005 International Price Comparison, in which various African countries had to price a 2003 or 2004 bottle of Bordeaux, a particular front loading washing machine, and a Peugeot 407 with air conditioning (Deaton and Aten 2014: 18). Measuring PPP is fraught with difficulties then, though of course similar problematic methodologies used across time might still help us to identify trends, including falling absolute poverty numbers.

Nonetheless, there are serious questions of reliability in global poverty figures.

More problematic is the argument that "globalisation" or the simple embrace of market friendly policies is the reason why poverty has fallen. As we saw above this was an argument made by Jim O' Neill and is central to his BRICs and rising South story. In terms of causality, this argument was also made by the World Bank (2002) report *Globalization, Growth and Poverty*. There are serious problems with this report and the wider argument about globalisation (Kiely 2008; 2015: Chap. 6). Briefly, the way that globalisation or market friendly policies are used as proxies for measuring openness in the world economy is seriously flawed, and there are countries with a history of greater openness than both China and India which have not experienced rapid growth. Indeed, if we measure trade policy indicators such as average tariff rates, then the Bank's own data suggest that if we measure openness not by trade/GDP ratios or changes in these ratios since 1975, and instead focus on trade and investment policies in 1997, allegedly high globalisers had higher average tariffs (35 %) than low globalisers (20 %) (Sumner 2004: 1174). Thus, O' Neill's case for some kind of straightforward causal relationship between globalisation and poverty reduction is not clearly established.

More important however, if we consider in greater depth the relationship between national inequality and both global inequality and absolute poverty, a much darker picture emerges. We can do so by examining in more detail some of the most recent data, based on the 2011 International Price Comparison. Two favoured new measures for absolute poverty are either $1.44 or $1.78, again adjusted to take account of PPP. Based on provisional estimates, the $1.44 figure gives us a count of 449 million living in absolute poverty, while the $1.78 figure puts the headcount at 745 million (Edward and Sumner 2015: 33). However a common criticism is that both of these benchmarks are far too low, as if someone living on, say, $1.79 a day in the USA would not be living in absolute poverty. Some have suggested a $2 measure, whereby the headcount increases to 963 billion. But again is someone living on $2.01 a day in the USA not living in absolute poverty? Thus, $2.50 gives us a figure of 1.45 billion, but again this might still be too low. If we then shift the figure to $10 a day, we have a massive headcount of 4.7 billion people (Edward and Sumner 2015: 33). Now of course $10 a day is a world away from the lower figures of $1.25 to $2.50 a day, where the debate usually takes place, and indeed much of the debate about a global middle class identifies those as people living on more than $10 a day. Nor do these measures tell us about trends, and whether the numbers on $2.50 or $10 a day is declining over a period of time.

But there are a number of responses to these objections. First, even if there is a downward trend in poverty numbers, this does not establish causality in terms of "globalisation friendly policies," for reasons already discussed. Moreover, such downward trends existed in periods before neoliberal globalisation. This is a problem for the liberal internationalist and especially the neoliberal arguments concerning globalisation. Second, it is the case that even $2.50 is a very low benchmark—thus to further stretch the examples used above, if we consider the PPP figure for the USA, this would be US$2.50, and a figure just above that does not sound like one where an American citizen would be lifted out of absolute poverty. Third, and related to this point, even a slight shift in income for people living in poverty could translate to a massive downward measurement in poverty numbers, a point reinforced by the methodological issues addressed above. For this reason Pritchett (2006) argues that there has not been a significant reduction in poverty so much as a shift in the *degree of poverty*. This brings us closer to the heart of the argument concerning globalisation, the rising South and inequality, for this point applies above all to those living just above the $2.50 line but below the $10 line. Even if there are "only" 1.5 billion people living in absolute poverty, there are 3 billion more people close to or at risk of falling back into absolute poverty. Fourth, and following on from the third point, almost all of those living below $2.50 and (to a slightly lesser extent) the $10 measure live in the global South. According to the International Labour Organization (ILO), insecure employment has increased so that it constitutes 19.9% of the labour force in high income countries, but as much as 84.1% of the labour force in middle income countries (ILO 2015). This is not then the modernisation story of global convergence.

Now of course the convergence/modernisation/neoliberal/liberal internationalism story might respond that there is a long way to go, but the fact that the South has risen and absolute poverty has fallen shows that we are moving in the right direction. Implicit in this argument—and explicit in O' Neill's distinction between inequality and poverty (above)—is the view that poverty is a residual phenomenon which will be resolved by growth, which in turn will occur through globalisation friendly policies. We have already dealt with the question of causality and globalisation friendly policies, but what can be added to this argument is an assessment of inequality trends and how these have impacted on poverty. In the period from around 1945 to 1990, most of the poor were concentrated in the poorest developing countries of the South, or what we now call the least developed countries. This is no longer the case. Based on earlier World Bank data, Kanbur and Sumner (2012: 688) estimate that between 71 % and 76 % of the world's poor live in middle income countries (850–950 million people), while between 24 % and 29 % (350 million people) live in low income countries, mainly in sub-Saharan Africa. China and India (both middle income countries) accounted for half of the world's poor in 2007–08, compared to around 66 % in 1990. However, this is not the whole story as there is a significant concentration of the world's poor in five middle income countries, namely, Pakistan, India, China, Nigeria and Indonesia (Kanbur and Sumner 2012: 688–9). More recent data (Edward and Sumner 2015: 33) broadly confirms this thesis that growth in middle income countries has left significant numbers of people behind.

Again, it might be argued by those propagating the centrality of convergence trends that this reflects the fact that some low income countries have moved up to middle income countries from 1990 to 2007–08, and that in time others will be lifted out of poverty. But an alternative account is that inequality matters and has a serious impact of the level of poverty reduction. Whereas in the past poverty was more concentrated in low income countries where almost everyone was poor, and therefore the residual account of poverty might have been more plausible (though there may still have been relational causes operating at a global level), the geography of global poverty today suggests that a relational account which highlights inequality is more convincing. Sumner (2016) estimates that if the consumption of a person on PPP $2.50 a day grows at an annual rate of consumption growth from 1990 to 2012, then it will take almost 130 years to get up to PPP $10 a day. Global convergence thus seems a very long way away. Furthermore, the shift from boom to bust in emerging markets means that the annual rate of both economic and consumption growth that took place for 1990–2012 is unlikely to be repeated, which puts the $10 a day threshold even further back than 130 years. Thus, for example, Brazil's booming economy helped finance the government's redistribution polices through conditional cash transfers, but the shift to economic crisis has severely undermined this programme.

## Conclusion: Global Inequality and the Rise of the South

Much of the rising South thesis—particularly among those optimists who see it as an opportunity for all—is linked to the idea that there is a new global middle class. *The Economist* has even talked on a "new bourgeoisie" of 2.5 billion people. However, this global middle class amounts to people living on a figure as low as $10 a day, adjusted for PPP. In actual fact around 71 % of humanity live on less than $10 a day, and $10 a day amounts to $3650 a year in the USA, which hardly amounts to membership of a global middle class, let alone a new bourgeoisie (Hart-Landsberg 2015). The value of the real living standard equivalent for a family of four in the USA has been estimated to be $29,200 a year, and only 13% of humanity enter this category (and which itself can hardly be called middle class). It goes without saying, as the data presented in this chapter show, that most of this 13% live in the North, and this is perhaps the main reason that we can talk of the persistence of cores and peripheries in the world economy, and in many respects these still overlap with the global North–South divide. Of course there are rich elites in the global South, but growing inequality within most countries means that there is little chance that many will become part of a middle class in the foreseeable future. Oxfam's (2016) latest report on inequality usefully puts this into perspective, and it estimates that in 2015 the wealth of 62 individuals is the same as the wealth of 3.6 billion people. In 2010 the first figure referred to 388 individuals, rather than 62. In the same period, the wealth of the richest 62 has risen by 44 % while the wealth of the bottom 50% fell by 41 %. The optimistic scenario concerning the rise of the South and a rising middle class is not convincing.

## References

Akyuz, Y. 2012. The Staggering Rise of the South? South Centre Research Paper no. 44, Geneva, pp. 1–54.

Chen, S., and M. Ravallion. 2012. Absolute Poverty Measures for the Developing World, 1981 to 2008. In *Measuring the Real Size of the World Economy*, ed. World Bank, 531–552. Washington: World Bank.

Deaton, A., and B. Aten. 2014. Trying to Understand the PPPs in ICP 2011. NBER Working Paper no. 20244, Washington.

Edward, P., and A. Sumner. 2013. The Geography of Inequality: Where and How Much Has Income Distribution Changed since 1990. Center for Global Development Working Paper no. 341, Washington, pp. 1–42.

Edward, P., and A. Sumner. 2015. New Estimates of Global Poverty and Inequality: How Much Difference Do Price Data Really Make? Center for Global Development Working Paper, Washington.
Hart-Landsberg, M. 2015. Signs of Global Slowdown. http://blogs.lclark.edu/hart-landsberg/category/china/. Accessed 14 Jan 2016.
ILO. 2015. *World Employment and Social Outlook*. Geneva: ILO.
Kanbur, R., and A. Sumner. 2012. Poor Countries or Poor People? *Journal of International Development* 24(6): 686–695.
Kiely, R. 2008. Poverty through "Insufficient Exploitation and/or Globalization"? Globalized Production and New Dualist Fallacies. *Globalizations* 5(3): 419–432.
Kiely, R. 2015. *The BRICs, US 'Decline' and Global Transformations*. London: Palgrave.
Nayyar, D. 2009. Developing Countries in the World Economy: The Future in the Past? Annual Lecture 12, United Nations University World Institute for Development Economics Research, Helsinki, pp. 1–46.
Nayyar, D. 2013. *Catch Up*. Oxford: Oxford University Press.
Nolan, P. 2012. *Is China Buying the World?* Cambridge: Polity.
OECD. 2010. *Perspectives on Global Development, 2010, Shifting Wealth*. Paris: OECD Development Centre.
O' Neill, J. 2013. *The Growth Map*. London: Portfolio Penguin.
Oxfam. 2016. An Economy for the 1%. Oxfam Briefing Paper no. 210. https://www.oxfam.org/sites/www.oxfam.org/files/file_attachments/bp210-economy-one-percent-tax-havens-180116-en_0.pdf. Accessed 31 Jan 2016.
Pritchett, L. (2006) 'who is not Poor? Dreaming of a World Truly Free of Poverty', *World Bank Research Observer* 21(1): 1–24.
Reddy, S. 2007. Death in China. *New Left Review* 45(2): 49–65.
Sumner, A. 2004. Epistemology and "Evidence" in Development Studies: A Review of Dollar and Kraay. *Third World Quarterly* 25(6): 1167–1177.
Sumner, A. 2016. *Global Poverty: Deprivation, Distribution and Development since the Cold War*. Oxford: Oxford University Press.
UNCTAD. 2012. *Trade and Development Report 2012*. Geneva: UNCTAD.
UNDP. 2013. *Human Development Report 2013*. New York: UNDP.
World Bank. 2002. *Globalization, Growth and Poverty*. Oxford: Oxford University Press.

CHAPTER 6

# Conclusion: Theorising the Changing Global North–South Divide

**Abstract** This chapter revisits the questions outlined in Chap. 2 in the light of the data, evidence and analysis presented in Chaps. 3 through to 5. The argument is that the evidence presented confirms more closely to "the dependency story" than the modernisation theory—and that therefore (in contrast to liberal internationalism and neoliberalism) we can still talk of cores and peripheries within global capitalism. The chapter then revisits the problems of dependency approaches and in doing so examines in more depth the concept of uneven and combined development, and how this might be used to reflect more widely on both the rise and fall of the South.

Current usages of this concept—to explain geopolitical conflict—are rejected. Instead, the concept is utilised to recognise the reality of diffusion—the South is not stagnant but is changing—but also that this diffusion is uneven and therefore not leading to anything like convergence. Finally, this is emphasised by summarising once again the shift from emerging markets boom to emerging markets crisis, with particular attention paid to the fate of the concept of the BRICs, and its own rise and fall at Goldman Sachs.

**Keywords** US power • Uneven and combined development • Emerging markets crisis



R. Kiely, *The Rise and Fall of Emerging Powers*,
DOI 10.1007/978-3-319-34012-8_6

This concluding chapter brings the arguments of the previous chapters together, and further develops one concept which has so far only been alluded to—that of uneven and combined development. The chapter starts by briefly reviewing the question of US power and international relations (IR) theory. It is suggested here that the concept of interdependence is important and goes some way towards capturing the specific nature of US power in the post-1945 world, and that this is an important part of the story of the "rise and fall" of the South in recent years. The chapter then moves on to reconsider development theory—and the idea of modernisation and dependency—in light of the rise of the South, and its fall. While holding on to the idea that modernisation and dependency are useful as framing devices, as used throughout this book, the section then reminds the reader of the flaws associated with both perspectives, namely, the tendency towards overgeneralisation. The section warns of the dangers of replicating these errors now, so that the "rise" of the South was one-sidedly seen as evidence supporting modernisation and convergence, and so the "fall" of the South may see a return to the one-sided stagnationist thesis associated with some versions of dependency theory, and underdevelopment theory in particular. While the section still gives support to the concept of dependency, the third section then introduces the idea of uneven and combined development. While briefly taking issue with some of the ways in which this approach has been used in IR theory in recent years, the third section shows how this might be useful in accounting for elements of both convergence and divergence in the international order, including the arguments concerning the rise and fall of the South. Finally, section four completes the book by summarising again the reasons why we are now shifting from an emerging markets boom discourse to one that focuses more on an emerging markets crisis.

## US Power and IR Theory Revisited

The rise and fall of the South should be located within a wider understanding of the nature of US hegemony and the political economy of contemporary globalisation. Moving beyond a focus on the last 15 years, we need to recognise how the US state has been central to the regulation of an increasingly global capitalism and since 1945 taken the lead in the promotion of a liberal international order (Panitch and Gindin 2012: 112–22), with increasingly open borders in terms of foreign investment. The USA has played the leading role in the promotion of this order with the support of other capitalist states, both before and after the Cold War. The crisis of the 1970s led to the first wave of talk about US decline (Mandel 1970; Gilpin 1975) but such analyses failed to see how US hegemony was inseparable from the creation of a global capitalism (Strange 1987). Rather than US decline, we saw the intensification *both* of the liberal international order and of US hegemony, so that by 1999, the real GDP of the USA was 20 % higher than that of the top 12 European countries, compared to relative parity in 1982 (Panitch and Gindin 2005: 151). While the late 1980s and early 1990s saw a further wave of talk about US decline (Kennedy 1989; Arrighi 1994), in fact this was the start of a new period of dominance as the Soviet Union and its allies collapsed and Japan entered a period of low growth and deflation. What followed was the "long boom" of the 1990s, the subject of this book, which lasted from around 1992 to 2007–08, and it was in this era that we saw the emergence of a new South. Some realists and world systems theorists then suggested that with the crisis of 2008, this new South led by China would challenge the USA which was said to be in decline (Layne 2009; Pape 2009; Subrammanian 2011; and see Chap. 2). But as should by now be clear, this new South has not "decoupled" from the West, and the USA in particular. The South did recover more rapidly than the developed world after 2009, but this was due to the success of fiscal stimuli programmes, continued relatively high commodity prices and capital inflows from the North, in part facilitated by quantitative easing policies (Chap. 4). Furthermore, within this order, US deficits should not necessarily be considered signs of intrinsic weakness, as theorists of hegemonic decline contend. As we have seen, this argument fails to capture significant changes in the international order since 1945, particularly the significance of the internationalisation of capital (Chap. 3), and the leading role of US capital in that process (Chaps. 3 and 4). The implication should be clear—the US state is playing a leading role in the promotion and regulation not only of US capital, but of *global* capital. The crisis does not change this, as states turned to the USA to play a leading role in finding ways out of the crisis. This wider argument is not dissimilar to some versions of liberal internationalism (Ikenberry 2014; Nye 2011, 2015; Beckley 2011/2012; and see Chap. 2) and theorists of globalisation (Held et al. 1999) and transnational capitalism (Robinson 2004). But as we have seen, states are the agents as well as the victims of "globalisation," and the US state remains the most powerful state in the international order. Moreover, US capital continues to play a leading role in the global economy, and other parts of the world are in many ways in a subordinate position within global production networks (Chaps. 3 and 4).

This argument thus draws heavily on the work of Panitch and Gindin (2012). On the other hand, it might be argued that their work implies that US hegemony leads to a progressive diffusion of capitalism throughout the globe, as though US imperialism was the progressive pioneer of capitalism (see Warren 1980). Thus, in keeping with the spirit of Panitch and Gindin's work (and see Panitch and Gindin 2012: 211–20, 283–92), we need to examine continued hierarchy in the international order—the uneven and unequal forms of integration which have been the subject of this book. Put more specifically, we need to be careful not to conflate—as liberal internationalists and neoliberals do—the development of capitalism with integration into the world economy, and to be clearer on the uneven and unequal integration of states into the international order (and the different forms of capitalism in that order). We therefore need to look again at the question of development.

## Rising South, Globalisation and Development Theory Revisited: Modernisation and Dependency

So far then we have suggested that the rising South thesis needs to be situated in the context of changes in the nature of global capitalism, which involves an affinity with notions of interdependence and globalisation. In many respects these ideas undermine theories which emphasise cycles of hegemonic advance and decline, such as some versions of realism and world systems theory. But at the same time, this does not necessarily mean that we should endorse liberal internationalist theories, and still less neoliberal approaches to development. Chapter 4 highlighted some of the limitations of the rise of the South through an examination of corporate power, and showed how the rise of Chinese companies is largely confined to the Chinese market, and the rise of Chinese exports largely reflects China's (subordinate) role in the globalisation of production through global production networks. China's sheer size and foreign exchange reserves of course means that its rise is significant, and China is the main foreign creditor for US debt, and its development has led to favourable economic spin-offs for some countries in the South. However, in terms of the former, continued purchase of US debt, especially by official sources after the financial crisis, shows the extent to which China is integrated into the US-led liberal international order, and in terms of the latter there are costs for the South (deindustrialisation and excessive dependence on primary commodities). These costs were partly hidden during the boom years before the financial crisis, and in the Chinese-led recovery from 2010, but they have become increasingly visible as commodity price increases have slowed or reversed. Moreover, much of the boom in the South after 2010 was also a product of the inflow of foreign investment from the global North, which has fuelled speculation and consumption but not production, and which can easily be exported back to the North.

In this regard we might argue that dependency remains a useful concept for understanding the specific conditions of late capitalist development (Palma 1978; Larrain 1989). Under these conditions, late development may take the form of continued dependence on the established capitalist powers, in the form of dependence on (both financial and productive) capital, Western markets and foreign technology (see Sutcliffe 1971). In the discussion in Chaps. 3 and 4, it was clear that in some respects the emerging powers remain dependent in at least some of these ways. We have seen how much of the boom in the South since the early 2000s rests on demand for primary goods, though the increase in demand is accounted for more by China, another emerging power. At the same time, however, China itself remains an economy dependent in some respects on the export of manufactured goods, as well as on the wider investment decisions of multinational capital using sourcing strategies in global production networks. Emerging powers maintained high growth rates both before and after the 2008 financial crisis, in part through capital inflows, and in many respects were the beneficiaries of the quantitative easing policies introduced by governments in response to the crisis. Now of course the USA is also dependent on capital flows in order to finance its deficits, which might be taken as evidence of interdependence in the international order, rather than the one-sided dependence of some states or capitals on others. But it should be clear from the argument made in Chaps. 3 and 4 that the US dependence on foreign capital has different consequences from other countries' dependence on US capital, and specifically US foreign investment is far more profitable on the whole than foreign investment into the USA. This observation is all the more true if we are making the stronger claim that a process of transformation is taking place in the international order. For if such a transformation is taking place, then we would expect the emerging powers to have powerful, diverse economies that can compete with the already established economies, not only in older sectors, but in the new, most dynamic sectors as well. While there has been some successes in this regard, the data cited in earlier chapters on research and development, triadic patents and global competiveness show the limits of this so-called transformation. Furthermore, as Chap. 5 showed, the nature of inequality is such that those living in absolute poverty are almost all located in the developing world, and those just above this level and still suffering high levels of insecurity are far more likely to live in the developing world than in the developed world.

There is, however, one possible problem with drawing on the modernisation versus dependency debate to help us understand the rising South thesis. Implicit in the rising South thesis in recent years has been some notion of modernisation, or perhaps more accurately, convergence in terms of the global North–South divide. While most of this material expresses some degree of qualification, it is still the case that much of the rising South thesis was excessively optimistic about the development prospects of the South as a whole. In other words, it overgeneralised in ways that paralleled earlier modernisation theories. On the other hand, this book has argued that we are now moving into an era where we are likely to see far more attention paid to a crisis in the South. The danger then is that an excessive pessimism may replace the excessive optimism of the boom years. This is likely to be combined with a distinctly anti-dependency approach in which Western-dominated neoliberal explanations which argue that the South is insufficiently liberalised, often by the same writers and organisations that explained the rise of the South through liberalisation. But even among more radical approaches, dependency approaches may well make a comeback. In one respect this is no bad thing, but there is the danger then of regarding the developing world as doomed to stagnation, as underdevelopment theory earlier contended. This again points us to the problems of overgeneralisation as suggested in Chap. 2. The theoretical origins of underdevelopment theory are rooted in an understanding of not only peripheral capitalism, but *all capitalisms*, as tending towards stagnation (see Baran 1957; Baran and Sweezy 1966), which simply flies in the face of the continued dynamism (as well as insecurity, marginalisation and exploitation) of contemporary capitalism, including in the periphery. This point holds even though the contemporary international order has seen a period of lower growth since the financial crisis, something that seems set to continue for a considerable period of time.

But more specifically, it is one thing to recognise subordination in the international order, but quite another to conflate this with absolute stagnation. The international order faces a series of significant challenges in the years ahead, and these are particularly acute for the global South, much of which is entering a period of lower or negative growth. The reasons why the problems are so acute for the South include its relative marginalisation, subordination and dependence in the international order, which its "rise" did not eradicate. But recognising all of this is not the same as suggesting that—like 1960s underdevelopment theory—the South is set on a course of ongoing and inevitable stagnation for the foreseeable future. This is so, for we also have to recognise that, albeit in unequal ways, there has been some diffusion of capitalism across the globe, and the period from the early 1990s to 2008 and beyond was a significant example of this. This is precisely the fact of interdependence that is central to the liberal internationalist IR tradition, and this is the kernel of truth in the modernisation thesis. But the limits of this must also be recognised, as the dependency thesis suggests. So in some respects then we need an approach which recognises both diffusion and divergence. This is considered in the next section.

## The Global North–South Divide and Uneven and Combined Development

Recent Marxist-inspired debates in IR have drawn on the idea of uneven and combined development, associated with Trotsky (1970). Trotsky developed this idea to problematise the idea that the diffusion of capitalism throughout the world would lead to the "backward" nations following a path of development similar to that of the "advanced" nations. In the case of Russia, it integrated into the world economy in such a way that some degree of capitalist industrialisation occurred (diffusion), but coincided with backward forms that were not destroyed by capitalist penetration (divergence) (Trotsky 1977: 27–28). Trotsky increasingly developed this theory, to analyse both world history and the ways in which capitalism intensified these processes. There was some degree of capitalist diffusion:

> In contrast to the economic systems that preceded it, capitalism inherently and constantly aims at economic expansion, at the penetration of new territories, the surmounting of economic differences, the conversion of self-sufficient provincial and national economies into a system of financial interrelationships. Thereby it brings about their rapprochement and equalizes the economic and cultural levels of the most progressive and the most backward countries. (Trotsky 1970: 18)

But there were also tendencies that hindered diffusion in any straightforward way:

> By drawing the countries economically closer to one another and levelling out their stages of development, capitalism, however, operates by methods of its own, that is to say, by anarchistic methods which constantly undermine its own work, set one country against another, and one branch of industry against another, developing some parts of world economy while hampering and throwing back the development of others. (Trotsky 1970: 19)

Much of this debate has been used to partly defend classical Marxist theories of imperialism and suggest that the state system—and ongoing geopolitical competition between states in an uneven capitalist world—is bound to be competitive and prone to rivalry as it "sets one country against another" (see Anievas 2010; for a critique, see Kiely 2010). The problem with this argument is that uneven and combined development takes place within as well as between nation-states so one cannot simply map uneven accumulation onto the state system and then read off from that the centrality of geopolitical rivalry between states, just as anarchy in realist thought is an insufficient approach for understanding conflict between states.

However, uneven and combined development *can* help us to point to ongoing hierarchies and inequalities which are not reducible to class in the international order. Using uneven and combined development in this way can lead one to reject the idea of a static North–South divide (dependency theory's weakness), but also to recognise that a simple convergence between countries is not happening, even with the rise of China and the BRICs (dependency theory's strength). This has enormous political implications in terms of understanding contemporary interdependence, because developing countries are integrated into the international order on highly unequal terms, and so-called free trade policies serve to undermine processes of capitalist development. In this way we have an imperialism of free trade which kicks away the (developmental) ladder from late developers. Indeed, the liberal internationalist analysis of US hegemony can in part be regarded as a project designed to show how an open door policy works in the interest of the USA (see Beckley 2011/2012). In other words, uneven and combined development can usefully capture the reality of global capitalist diffusion, but also show how this both "equalizes the economic and cultural levels of the most progressive and the most backward countries" and simultaneously develops "some parts of world economy while hampering and throwing back the development of others" (Trotsky 1970: 19).

This does not of course mean that US hegemony has not been challenged in some respects in recent years. Hegemony is not reducible to economic factors, and US leadership has been challenged by social and political movements and governments in parts of the South, and by state representatives in international institutions. This book has, however, suggested that the significance of economic sources supposedly challenging US hegemony has been exaggerated. Furthermore, in order to understand the specificity of US hegemony, we must move beyond a methodological nationalism which reduces the US economy to national shares of global GDP or trade and budget deficits, and examine the close connection between economic globalisation and US leadership. None of this of course means that the situation will remain static or that BRIC countries, or the South more generally, simply passively accepts all of the characteristics of the current international order. It is undoubtedly the case that the BRIC countries' domestic deployment of market friendly policies is selective (Rucki 2011; Strange 2011; Breslin 2013; Stephen 2014; Kiely 2015: Chap. 3). Nonetheless, to date this has not led to a significant challenge to the nature of the US-led liberal international order (Breslin 2013: 629; Kiely 2015: Chap. 7). This is not to say that the USA does not face enormous difficulties in the current period (Gamble 2014), and one even might make a strong case for saying that US hegemony is in decline because of the questionable capacity of the US state to manage the fallout from the financial crisis of 2008. This question is given an added urgency at the time of writing, in February 2016, when potential presidential candidates for both the Democrats and Republicans open up all kinds of possibilities, albeit for very different reasons. But focusing on US state capacity in this way is not the same thing as saying that the USA is in decline because of the rise of China and other major countries in the global South, not least because US state incapacity vis-à-vis the crisis is a problem for these countries as much if not more than for the USA. To take one illustrative example, the Asian Infrastructure Investment Bank was officially launched in January 2016. In the planning stage, the USA lobbied some key allies (Japan, South Korea and Australia) not to join, but, following Britain's lead, many countries joined. On the face of it, this looks like a sign of US weakness, but in fact there are two deeper factors that need to be considered. First, in some respects the bank's formation constitutes a retreat on the part of China, in response to criticisms of their bilateral aid practices in much of the global South. Seen in this light, the multilateral bank represents a retreat from bilateral practices which were often accused of neo-colonialism (see Hung 2016). But more important, whatever the US reasons for opposing the bank's formation, the bank needs the inclusion of Western powers to enhance its credit rating, and most important of all, like the BRICS development bank, investment in Asian infrastructure will be financed through a number of sources, including the World Bank and the Asian Development Bank and so the new bank's loans are likely to complement rather than challenge these sources (Starrs 2016: 101–2). Once again then we should see such developments in terms of the making of a global capitalism, rather than through the lens of perceived zero-sum games between national states. The final section reflects further on these issues in the light of the growing crisis of the global South.

## Emerging Markets and the North–South Divide: From Boom to Bust

This short book has argued that the rising South discourse of recent years is now likely to give way to a discourse which focuses on a growing slowdown or even crisis in much of the Global South. This shift towards an emerging markets crisis can be considered a third stage of the financial crisis, following the subprime and Eurozone crisis of 2008 and 2010. The first saw capital inflows and cheap credit fuelling a subprime boom which, when accompanied by the securitisation of financial products, eventually turned to bust. Much the same occurred following cheap capital flows from the core of the Eurozone to its periphery. The third stage saw cheap money leave the North for the South, but this too is now coming to an end. Those who argued that the crisis represented a crisis only for the West underestimated both the conditions which gave rise to the boom before 2008 and the short-term reasons for the recovery of much of the South from 2010 onwards. In particular, the post-crisis rise of the South is now unravelling as China's export-led model and investment boom have slowed, capital inflows to the South are increasingly becoming outflows, and commodity prices are stagnating or falling sharply. Added to that are downgrades in growth forecasts (particularly acute among Brazil, Russia and China—see UN 2016), growing emerging market debt (not necessarily a problem but it becomes one when combined with lower growth rates), the fact that in some cases debt is denominated in US dollars (and so falling local currencies increase the debt burden), rising current account and budget deficits among some countries (especially in Latin America) and the impact of the BRIC countries on the South as a whole (from a 2011–13 peak, African trade with China has almost halved), then we can indeed identify a shift from boom to bust (Klasa 2015). This is not to say that a crisis along the lines of the 1997 Asian financial crisis or even the 1982 Latin American debt crisis is inevitable, and many developing countries (above all China) have attempted to protect themselves from potential difficulties. In particular, many have built up foreign exchange reserves to protect their economies. But, as this book has demonstrated, the rise of the South did not reflect an international transformation in which they were no longer dependent on or subordinate to the global North. And this "rise" has now given way to a "fall" in which their continued subordination will leave many countries—and peoples—deeply exposed, in and through the uneven and combined development of the international order. This is perhaps best represented—symbolically at least—by the fate of the Goldman Sachs BRIC fund. Chapter 2 showed how the BRIC acronym was coined by Jim O' Neill when an employee of Goldman Sachs. In 2007 a BRIC investment fund was established. In 2015 the fund was closed following an 88 % loss in assets since its peak in 2010 (Bloomberg 2016). For the investment fund that coined the term, the BRIC era is over. Much the same can be said about the supposed rise of the South.

## References


Anievas, A. (ed.). 2010. *Marxism and World Politics.* London: Routledge.

Arrighi, G. 1994. *The Long Twentieth Century.* London: Verso.

Baran, P. 1957. *The Political Economy of Growth.* New York: Monthly Review Press.

Baran, P., and P. Sweezy. 1966. *Monopoly Capital.* New York: Monthly Review Press.

Beckley, M. 2011/2012. China's Century? *International Security* 36(3): 41–78.

Bloomberg. 2016. Goldman's BRIC Era Ends as Fund Folds. http://www.bloomberg.com/news/articles/2015-11-08/goldman-s-bric-era-ends-as-fund-closes-after-years-of-losses. Accessed 15 Feb 2016.

Breslin, S. 2013. China and the Global Order: Signalling Threat or Friendship? *International Affairs* 89(3): 615–663.

Gamble, A. 2014. *Crisis without End?* Basingstoke: Palgrave.

Gilpin, R. 1975. *US Power and the Multinational Corporation*. New York: Basic Books.

Held, D., A. McGrew, D. Goldblatt, and J. Perraton. 1999. *Global Transformations*. Cambridge: Polity.

Hung, H.F. 2016. *The China Boom: Why China Will Not Rule the World*. Cambridge: Harvard University Press.

Ikenberry, G.J. 2014. The Logic of Order: Westphalia, Liberalism and the Evolution of International Order in the Modern Era. In *Power, Order and Change in World Politics*, ed. G.J. Ikenberry, 83–106. Cambridge: Cambridge University Press.

Kennedy, P. 1989. *The Rise and Fall of the Great Powers*. New York: Fontana.

Kiely, R. 2010. *Rethinking Imperialism*. Basingstoke: Palgrave.

Kiely, R. 2015. *The BRICs, US 'Decline' and Global Transformations*. London: Palgrave.

Klasa, A. 2015. Chinese Investment in Africa Plunges 83%. *Financial Times*, October 21.

Larrain, J. 1989. *Theories of Development*. Cambridge: Polity.

Layne, C. 2009. The Waning of US Hegemony—Myth or Reality? A Review Essay. *International Security* 34(1): 147–172.

Mandel, E. 1970. *Europe versus America?* London: New Left Books.

Nye, J. 2011. *The Future of Power*. New York: Public Affairs.

Nye, J. 2015. *Is the American Century Over?* Cambridge: Polity.

Palma, G. 1978. Dependency and Development: A Formal Theory of Underdevelopment or a Methodology for the Analysis of Concrete Situations of Underdevelopment? *World Development* 6: 881–924.

Panitch, L., and S. Gindin. 2005. Euro-Capitalism and American Empire. In *Varieties of Capitalism, Varieties of Approaches*, ed. D. Coates, 139–159. Basingstoke: Palgrave.

Panitch, L., and S. Gindin. 2012. *The Making of Global Capitalism*. London: Verso.

Pape, R. 2009. Empire Falls. *National Interest* 99: 21–34.

Robinson, B. 2004. *A Theory of Global Capitalism*. Baltimore: Johns Hopkins University Press.

Rucki, S. 2011. Global Economic Crisis and China's Challenge to Global Hegemony: A Neo-Gramscian Approach. *New Political Science* 33(3): 335–355.

Starrs, S. 2016. BRICS—New Shareholders in the Global Capitalist System. *R/evolutions* 3(1): 96–118.

Stephen, M. 2014. Rising Powers, Global Capitalism and Liberal Global Governance: A Historical Materialist Account of the BRICs Challenge. *European Journal of International Relations* 20(4): 912–938.

Strange, S. 1987. The Persistent Myth of Lost Hegemony. *International Organization* 41(4): 551–574.

Strange, G. 2011. China's Post-Listian Rise: Beyond Radical Globalisation Theory and the Political Economy of Neoliberal Hegemony. *New Political Economy* 16(5): 539–559.

Subrammanian, A. 2011. The Inevitable Superpower: Why China's Rise Is a Sure Thing. *Foreign Affairs* 90(5): 66–78.

Sutcliffe, B. 1971. *Industry and Underdevelopment.* London: Addison-Wesley.

Trotsky, L. 1970. *The Third International after Lenin.* New York: Pathfinder, first published 1936.

Trotsky, L. 1977. *The History of the Russian Revolution.* London: Pluto, first published 1918.

UN. 2016. *World Economic Situations and Prospects 2016.* New York: UN.

Warren, B. 1980. *Imperialism: Pioneer of Capitalism.* London: Verso.

# Bibliography

Robinson, B. 2015a. The Fetishism of Empire: A Critical Review of Panitch and Gindin's the Making of Global Capitalism. *Studies in Political Economy* 93: 147–164.

Robinson, B. 2015b. The Transnational State and the BRICS: A Global Capitalism Perspective. *Third World Quarterly* 36(1): 1–21.



R. Kiely, *The Rise and Fall of Emerging Powers*,
DOI 10.1007/978-3-319-34012-8

# Index




R. Kiely, *The Rise and Fall of Emerging Powers*,
DOI 10.1007/978-3-319-34012-8

FSC
www.fsc.org
MIX
Papier | Fördert gute Waldnutzung
FSC® C083411

Kolibri 360 GmbH
Ferdinand-Jühlke-Straße 7
99095 Erfurt, Deutschland
produktsicherheit@kolibri360.de